FAITH MADE EASY

HAVE FAITH IN GOD

By LaRon D. Bennett Sr., DD

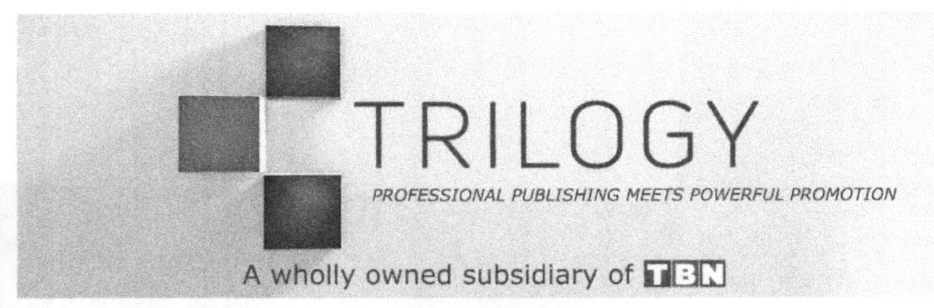

Faith Made Easy (Vol. 1 & Vol. 2)

Trilogy Christian Publishers A Wholly Owned Subsidiary of Trinity Broadcasting Network

2442 Michelle Drive Tustin, CA 92780

For information about special discounts for bulk purchases, please contact Trilogy Christian Publishing.

Manufactured in the United States of America

10 9 8 7 6 5 4 3 2 1

Library of Congress Cataloging-in-Publication Data is available.

ISBN: 978-1-68556-428-5

E-ISBN: 978-1-68556-429-2

DEDICATION

FCMI & Pastor Andrew "Andy" Velie

FCMI

I'm dedicating this book to my FCMI brothers and sisters and to a friend, brother, fellow FCMI member, and minister of the gospel, the late Pastor Andrew "Andy" Velie.

Many of my FCMI brothers and sisters have dedicated themselves to years of untold sacrifice for the Lord and the citizens of His kingdom.

The Fellowship of Churches and Ministers International (FCMI) was organized to provide churches and ministers with a way to work together in the kingdom of God to promote the work of our Lord Jesus Christ among the nations of the world.

It has been a blessing and an honor to get to know each of you and to call you all brethren. My prayer and hope is that we all finish strong.

Faith isn't confidence that you can do it; it is confidence that God will—or has—done it.

—LaRon D. Bennett Sr., DD

Andrew "Andy" Velie

To my friend and brother, Andrew "Andy" Velie. It's rare, even among the faithful, to meet someone with the depth of love, care, and devotion for the Lord and His people that Andy Velie had. Andy was a kind, gentle person and spirit. We connected the very first time we met. I greatly admired Andy; he personified Revelation 2:10. I am confident that he has been adorned with a crown of life from the Lord.

Andy spent an enormous amount of time in prayer and study of God's Word. He consistently displayed unconditional love for God and for God's people, no matter who they were or their status. Andy Velie truly was a man of God, devoted to God, ministry, and his family. He will be greatly missed.

TABLE OF CONTENTS

FOREWORD

Occasionally, when speaking with my then five-year-old grandson, Gabriel, he would tell me about his day. He may say something about a friend by saying, “Her take my paper, etc.” I would correct him, saying, “She took my paper, etc.” He did much better with math, but sometimes it was difficult to know whether he used memory to solve the problems or the principles underlying them.

Whether grammar or mathematics, I endeavored to teach him the concepts the subject was based upon, but if he was to master them, he would need to understand the principles that governed each. That’s true with everything we do in life.

We often seek to understand life’s concepts, the notions, thoughts, and ideas that are being conveyed. We seek life’s pictures, stopping there. We remember the words, then stop. Often, during life’s tests, we stop upon seeing the problems. The problem with not going beyond the concepts is that we rarely dig deep enough to learn and understand the principles that underlie them. The results of such an approach will be struggling through life and random failures.

To succeed in life and in everything we do, we must learn life’s principles and how to apply them. To become the master of anything, one must learn and understand the principles governing that thing. Everything has a basic principle that governs it as well as effecting principles that exert influence upon it. Learn a thing’s governing principles and its effecting principles; you will then be able to utilize it to benefit yourself and others.

This concept applies to everything in the Bible, including faith.

There are principles that govern faith, learn them, and F.A.I.T.H. will be made easy in your life.

This book will get you started down the road of understanding and applying the principles that govern faith. Learn them, learn to use them appropriately and with consistency. You will then become a great man or woman of faith.

Remember there are both natural and spiritual principles. If you are to succeed, you must learn them and learn how to appropriately apply both. Note, however, that spiritual principles transcend natural principles. Be sure never to allow a natural principle to limit the appropriate application of a spiritual principle.

Living life trying to solve problems without proper application of principles will leave you guessing. Guessing will eventually leave you frustrated. So it is with everything in God, so it is with faith. Learn and apply the principles of faith in everything you do. It will take time and patience, but you can do it. Doing so will help you succeed in all that you do. This book will help you. So get started; your life's result will depend on it.

And I gave my heart to seek and search out by wisdom concerning all things that are done under heaven: this sore travail hath God given to the sons of man to be exercised therewith. Ecclesiastes 1:13 (KJV)

Begin discovering and applying the principles that govern and affect the things you face. You will then see your life change in ways you cannot imagine.

AUTHOR'S NOTE

"For verily I say unto you, Till heaven and earth pass, one jot or one tittle shall in no wise pass from the law, till all be fulfilled"
(Matthew 5:18, KJV).

I pray you find as much joy, inspiration, and insight reading this book as I did writing it. I believe this book is inspired by the Lord to be written at this time to give His people a better understanding of faith and how they can and should use their faith in Him to impact their lives and the world.

The impetus for this book began when I received a call from the leader of a ministerial alliance asking me to share during an upcoming meeting.

Agreeing to do so, I asked the Lord to give me what He wanted me to share. He then gave me an outline for a topic on faith titled "Faith Made Easy." I then felt impressed to use the word "faith" as an acronym. He then gave me each word reflecting the acronym. I then created a handout based upon that acronym. It was so well received that I was impressed to write a mini-book to share the principles with others. Upon completing the draft of the mini-book, there were questions that convinced me of the importance of writing this first volume on this topic.

This first book is really two volumes in one broken into four sections. The first section being volume one, *Faith Made Easy: "Have Faith in God,"* gives a simple, straightforward approach to faith that can be used when walking in faith and serves as foundation and basis for the entire series. The remaining three sections comprise the second volume, *Faith Made Easy: "The*

Unveiling Of Faith," which unveils faith by shining a light upon faith that should help you see faith in ways that you may have never seen. Together, these volumes should help anyone to become a person of great, abiding faith.

Several things may be noticed while reading this book:

- The book is designed to be instructional. It's generally an easy read, but there are areas that are somewhat weighty, requiring more time and thought.
- References to God are capitalized, and references to the "devil" are lowercased.
- There are redundancies; some to cement certain points, and some to keep certain points fresh while reading.
- Great importance was given to word nuances, placing care and value upon each word.
- This book may challenge and provide insights that could only have been given by the Holy Spirit.

The goal of this book is to help the reader better understand and apply faith in every area of life. After reading it, I pray you will find that it's really not difficult to walk in faith and to have "faith in God."

—Pastor Dr. LaRon D. Bennet Sr., DD

PREFACE

I accepted Jesus Christ as my Lord and Savior in the summer of 1973. Since then, I have been taught many things about faith. Some of which helped me tremendously, and some did not.

Initially, I was taught that if I asked God for something, then asked again, I did not ask in faith, or I was doubting. For me, that was confusing.

Then there was the "Now Faith" movement that taught faith was present tense, *now*. They taught that whenever we asked in faith, we received what we asked right then. That is somewhat true, but in my mind, there was something lacking. Faith *is* present tense, but if I did not physically see what I asked God to materialize right then, does that mean that I didn't have faith? What about God's timing? What about God simply saying no?

There were several faith movements and teachings then and now. We even have those that reject the concept of faith altogether. But please don't get me wrong, I'm not saying that those teachings didn't have value; they did. I am saying, however, that to some extent, they left me confused, with a big "?" (question mark) between my ears. Looking back at those times, I discovered that what I lacked was detail and clarity. I'm sure there are many in the faith seeking that same detail and clarity; this book is designed to provide just that.

INTRODUCTION

"Now faith is the substance of things hoped
"for, the evidence of things not seen."
(Hebrews 11:1, KJV)

Hebrews 11:1 is probably the most quoted scripture on faith in the Bible. It may also be one of the most misunderstood.

At times, we all may struggle with that little five-letter word F.A.I.T.H. I, too, am challenged in this area of my walk with Christ. I'm certain that there will be times in every Christian's life when they will struggle in their walk of faith, but why?

I've wondered if I would have stood in faith as did first-century believers. They, like believers today, had to accomplish much by and through faith. They gave their lives and, many times, the lives of entire families in horrific ways while holding firm to their commitment and devotion to God.

I'm sure many who read this book have wondered the same thing. Would *I* have stood? Would *I* have continued to believe God? Would *I* have remained faithful? Would *I* have gone through? Would *I* have willingly suffered as those mentioned in Hebrews 11 and throughout the Scriptures?

We won't truly know that answer until we face the choices they faced. But if I had to guess, I believe that I and most of those that have given their lives to Christ will reach the same or similar conclusion as did they. Not being thrust into the situations earlier believers were thrust into is the reason for the uncertainty. On another level, however, we are faced with the same choices: believe God or not, stand or fall, hold fast or give in, have faith in

God or "*...curse God and die" (Job 2:9, KJV).*

Today's Christians (facing such situations) reach the same or similar conclusion. They, like Paul and so many others, conclude, "*...to live is Christ, but to die is gain" (Philippians 1:21, KJV).* This is not religious faith or fervor; it is a manifestation of pure, unadulterated "faith in God."

Too many believers approach faith as if there are two types of faith: One being varying levels of self-confidence; the second, a religious faith. They believe that God exists and is therefore worthy of devotion, worship, praise, and adoration. Such believers make efforts to please God by living "the best life they can" but conclude that they can't be perfect because they are but lowly sinners. They concede in advance that they will invariably sin because they can't help but do so. They then seemingly resolve that when they do, all will be well because they believe in God, and He loves them.

The early church did not have such an attitude toward faith. To them, there was only one faith: faith in God. The life they lived reflected that faith. Their lives reflected their confidence in and commitment to God. They either believed God, or they didn't. When they believed God, their confident commitment to Him was seamless. The expressions of their faith were seamless; they believed God and were willing to die in that belief.

The singularity of their belief in God was reflected in everything they did, including their belief that there was only one true and living God. They believed that if God said it, that settled it. Everything that they said and did reflected the depth of their faith in God.

Many believers struggle with that depth of faith because they do not understand faith. They do not recognize faith when they see it, even when manifested in their own lives. My goal is to also help believers know when they and others are walking in faith. I call this F.A.I.T.H. made easy.

"F.A.I.T.H." is an acronym for being "Focused," "Aggressive," "Intelligent," "Tenacious," and "Humble." When believers believe God for anything, they must ask themselves, *Am I focused, appropriately aggressive, operating in intelligence, tenacious, and humble?*

If you are walking in faith, in what or in whom is your faith directed? True faith is always rooted in and directed to God. Such faith will always require one to be focused, appropriately aggressive, intelligent, tenacious, and humble.

Jesus taught that having faith in God is a prerequisite to the implementation of faith. In this book, we will examine Jesus' teachings on faith. Jesus taught (in essence) that if you are going to do what seems to be impossible, you must have faith in God.

The key to making faith easy is to believe that God will do what He said that He would do, then conform your thoughts and actions to that belief. If you do that, faith will become easy. If you do that, you can stop reading this book now. If you want to understand better how to do that and see faith on a level you may have never seen before, keep reading, and I will show you how F.A.I.T.H. can be "made easy."

VOLUME 1:

HAVE FAITH IN GOD

SECTION 1

Faith is revealed in confidence in God, not in self-confidence. How confident in God are you? Your faith will hinge upon your answer to that question.

True faith is always:

Focused

Aggressive

Intelligent

Tenacious

Humble

...and is always placed in

and directed to God.

CHAPTER 1:

FAITH ABANDONED

"Nevertheless when the Son of man cometh, "shall he find faith on the earth?" (Luke 18:8, KJV)

Now the Spirit speaketh expressly, that in the latter times some shall depart from the faith, giving heed to seducing spirits, and doctrines of devils. 1 Timothy 4:1 (KJV)

When I first read Luke 18:8, I determined in my heart that when Jesus returns, He will find faith in my heart, even if He did not find it anywhere else on earth. I was a young nineteen-year-old zealous believer that believed that I could do anything. I believed that there was nothing impossible for me because there was nothing impossible for God. I was certain that I could do all things through Christ, who strengthened me.

Today, I still have that same faith. It has been tempered by the knowledge that comes with age, growth, and maturity. Things like: Is it God's will? Am I doing whatever I'm doing to honor God, myself, or others? Am I doing whatever I do in and under the power, might, and leading of the Holy Spirit? How will this impact God's relationship with me and others? Will those relationships be strengthened or diminished?

Jesus said that He did what He did through the Spirit of God

(Matthew 12:28). What is it about us that causes us to think that we can do on a whim anything that comes to our mind with or without any intervention from God? Or worse, assume that God will act on our behalf just because we have "the faith" that He will. "Heaven to you." He may not. Nor does He have to. He is God, and *you* just may be acting stupidly. God honors and acts in harmony with His Word. That's why it's so important to read, understand, and meditate upon God's Word. Doing so will help you to develop your relationship with God.

Too many believers fail to do that. I'm convinced that that is the main reason for much of the weakness and divisions we see in the church and in our lives. I believe such frailty is at least one of the reasons so many are departing from the faith.

One of the keys to great faith is developing the closeness with God that can only come with spending time with God and developing a personal, familial relationship with Him. Religious relationships will never get you there.

Today, many are abandoning their faith. They're falling like flies because their relationship with God is hollow, rooted in religion, not family. True, long-lasting family relationships are rooted in love.

Family relationships grow stronger in crisis. Those in the relationships are committed to one another because of their relationship with each other. The challenges and difficulties they encounter spur growth, causing them to *focus* on finding solutions. They will *aggressively* seek out those solutions and bring to bear the *intellectual* prowess to do so. They will be *tenacious* in their efforts to find their solutions, *humbly* submitting themselves as needed to get beyond the problem. Then, the next time, they do it all over again.

The great apostasy will occur among those that are out of relationship with God or are not in a familial relationship with God.

Ask any mom or dad if they would surrender their life for their children or each other. Ask the child that has a healthy, loving relationship with their parents if they would surrender their life for their parents. I believe, in most cases, the answer would be yes. Our heavenly Father set the example for us by giving His Son; in doing so, He was also giving Himself.

Those that abandon the family of God are likely not members of God's family. They may be religious, fair-weather Christians, but are they members of the family of the Most High God? Probably not.

"Many will say to me in that day, Lord, Lord, have we not prophesied in thy name? and in thy name have cast out devils? and in thy name done many wonderful works?" Matthew 7:22 (KJV)

"And then will I profess unto them, I never knew you: depart from me, ye that work iniquity." Matthew 7:23 (KJV)

True faith comes from God and is directed back to Him. If a person abandons their faith, they are abandoning their relationship with God. They are also abandoning family. Their actions make it clear that they either were never a part of the family of God or chose the family of the world and renounced the family of God. Simply put, you don't abandon family. In Christ, if you abandon your faith, you are really abandoning your family. In Matthew

7:23, Jesus is, in essence, saying, "You were never in relationship with me. You were not a member of my family."

The thing that keeps a family together is love. Every believer must take a Luke 10:27 (KJV) approach to their relationship with God, *"And he answering said, Thou shalt love the Lord thy God with all thy heart, and with all thy soul, and with all thy strength, and with all thy mind; and thy neighbour as thyself."*

If you love God with all of your heart, you will not deny Him; you *will* not abandon Him. Simply put, you don't abandon those you love. We've all heard the stories of those that used their bodies as shields to save those they loved. Jesus said that there is no greater expression of love than someone laying down their life for their friend (John 15:13). You don't abandon the ones you love.

So when people abandon "their faith," it is really an indication of the true position of their heart. That's why our faith must be placed squarely in the Lord. It's also why we place nothing between us and our relationship with God. Anything in our lives that stands between the Lord and us is in a vulnerable position. The devil will use whoever or whatever you value more than the Lord to get you to abandon not only your faith in God but also your relationship with God.

To have and maintain your faith in God and your relationship with God, you must love Him as family. If you do, you will never abandon Him, and you will never lose your faith in Him. It is also at that point when faith will truly become easy.

Things to Do to Not Abandon the Lord

- Love God with all of your heart.
- Never place anything between you and God.
- Resolve now that you will die for the Lord.
- Read and meditate on God's Word.
- Pray that the Lord will keep you and those you love from the hour of temptation and, if not, keep you in the hour of temptation.

CHAPTER 2:

FAITH MADE EASY

F.A.I.T.H. made easy is faith that is: "Focused," "Aggressive," "Intelligent," "Tenacious," and "Humble." When walking in faith, there will always be some combination of all five of those traits present and working harmoniously to accomplish the things being hoped for. Those five traits are indicators of the presence of faith and its intensity. Like making great music, bringing together focus, aggressiveness, intelligence, tenaciousness, and humility will work together to produce great faith. The following is an overview of the *acronym.*

Focused: True faith is always focused. A person walking in faith will always be focused. If you want to know whether you are walking in faith, ask yourself, "Am I focused?" Not focused on any old thing but focused on two things specifically: (1) focused on God and what He has said and (2) focused on the thing you are hoping for. Doing so will keep you on the path where you will see your hope become a reality.

Aggressive: The aggression that faith produces is faith's passion. True faith is always appropriately and sufficiently aggressive. The aggressiveness of faith will always bring to bear the passion, power, and energy necessary to plow through the inevitable challenges and obstacles that stand between you and the thing you are hoping for. Keep in mind, however, that the aggressiveness of faith is not a natural, carnal aggression. Carnal aggression is usually condescending and arrogant. Often, carnal aggression is an expression of insecurity. The aggressiveness of faith will never display such an emotion.

Intelligent: Faith will always operate intelligently. Intelligence, especially spiritual intelligence, will always be needed when accomplishing the things being "hoped for." True faith is not blind to facts or unaware of what is happening around it. Faith is not concerned with or controlled by events. It doesn't allow natural circumstances to dictate its response. Faith uses intelligence to navigate through circumstances in order to realize and accomplish the things being "hoped for."

Tenacious: True faith is always tenacious. When in faith, you will doggedly seek out ways to move toward the things being "hoped for" and do so in accordance with God's will. Faith without tenaciousness is not faith.

Humble: True faith is always humble. Humility gives faith its perspective. It balances personal needs, wants, and desires with the needs, wants, and desires of God and others. To be humble is to realize one's need for God. The humble selflessly, consistently, and totally trust God, believing that He will do what He said and (according to His will) give them the things "hoped for."

Humility facilitates the process for believers to walk in harmony with God, giving balance and a heart that is nimbly responsive to God's will. Humility enables the believer to, without question or hesitation, do what God wants. Those that are humble are reflexively obedient to God and render unquestionable service to Him.

Humble doesn't mean weakness; however, it does mean that

one realizes and acknowledges their need for God. Being humble in faith also means that you are not selfish, self-centered, or arrogant. True faith is never those things. Those walking in faith consider self, but not to the detriment of God, His will, and how their action will affect others. Those walking in humility operate under the principle of love. Love for God and loving others and loving self (Luke 10:27).

Note: F.A.I.T.H. is always active, never passive. At times faith may seem passive, but that perceived passivity is really active. Faith does what's necessary to reach the objective. As James said, "Show me your faith without your works; I will show you my faith by my works." Being Focused, Aggressive, Intelligent, Tenacious, and Humble are all indications that faith is at work.

Always Have Faith in God

"And Jesus answering saith unto
"them, Have faith in God."
Mark 11:22 (KJV)

For verily I say unto you, That
whosoever shall say unto this
mountain, Be thou removed, and
be thou cast into the sea; and shall
not doubt in his heart, but shall
believe that those things which he
saith shall come to pass; he shall
have whatsoever he saith.
Mark 11:23 (KJV)

Therefore I say unto you, What
things soever ye desire, when ye
pray, believe that ye receive them,
and ye shall have them.
Mark 11:24 (KJV)

CHAPTER 3:

HAVE FAITH IN GOD

For faith to truly become easy, it must always be placed in God. True faith is rooted in the confidence that *God* will—not that *we* can.

Faith in God is not today's Christianity's "God will" while we do nothing approach to faith. God is not our personal butler standing around waiting until we ask for something so that He can run and get it for us. That's childish, immature, ignorance of God, laziness. Faith's "God will" is confidence that God will honor His Word and do exactly what He said He would do. That is at the core of what faith in God is. Such faith is rooted in trust in God. Are your trust and confidence placed squarely in God? Not just trust in what God can or will do but trust in God the person. Our faith in God will be based upon our perception of God's character and abilities. God's abilities are not the determining factor of what He will or will not do, but His character is.

Trusting in God the person is the foundation of faith. If you don't trust God the person, it is unlikely that you will trust God the Creator. Lack of trust will make it impossible to have complete confidence in God and His word.

To build confidence in God's word, you must spend time with God the person. Doing so will help you to develop a personal relationship with God. Such a relationship can only come through experience. That means investing time in getting to know God on a personal level, not a religious one.

Relational Faith

Faith in God is relational. Our faith is a reflection and expression of our relationship with God. The less we know *Him,* the less we will trust Him, and the less faith we will have in Him. That was the message of Jesus to His disciples when He told them to "have faith in God." It is also His message to every believer today.

To grow in faith, believers must grow in their relationship with God. That can only be done by spending time with God. As we spend time with God, we will grow closer to Him. The closer we become in our relationship with God, the more we will get to know Him, and the more we will trust Him. We will not simply trust in Him as God; we will begin to trust in the person that God is. Doing that one thing will not only increase our faith; it will also transform our lives, and we will transform the lives of others. The apostle Saul is a great example of that.

Apostle Saul? Saul was the name of the apostle Paul before he met Jesus while traveling on the road to Damascus. At the time, Saul obviously had heard of Jesus but had no relationship with Him. If he had, he would not have been trying to destroy those that had such a relationship.

Saul was on his way to arrest Christians when he was blinded after being surrounded by a bright light. Falling to the ground, he heard a voice asking him, "…why are you persecuting Me?" In reply, Saul asked, "Who are You?" If Saul had a relationship with Jesus, he would have known the voice and would not have had to ask the question. Jesus answered, "I'm Jesus, the one you're persecuting." It was at that point that Saul was introduced to Christ. It was at that point Saul began his change and did so to the point where those whom he was once in league with sort to kill him. Read the full story in Acts 9:1–23.

Saul's Damascus Road experience was enough to introduce him to Christ, but an introduction does not make a relationship. All relationships begin with an introduction, but it's not enough to simply establish the relationship; the relationship must grow. To do that, Saul, now Paul, went to Arabia and spent three years getting to know God through studying the Scriptures and learning from God Himself (see Galatians 1:12–24).

Like Paul, we must not be satisfied with a simple introduction to Christ; that comes with the acceptance that He is real. Each of us must take the time to get to know Him on a personal level. To do that, we must learn Him. That takes time.

Every believer must take the time to develop a personal, intimate relationship with God and not filter that relationship through anyone or anything. Then, live a life of commitment and dedication to him. It is at that point when not only will their life change, but it will impact and change the lives of countless others for Christ.

Developing a personal, intimate relationship with God will produce trust in God. When we develop such a relationship, we will cease struggling with faith in God. Developing will take time, but that is true for any great relationship.

God Confident before Self-Confidence

Confidence in God is the key to faith. The modern approach to faith is rooted more in self-confidence than in being God-confident. That's the main reason the faith of many believers is so fragile. Modern-day believers' approach to faith is focused on not doubting. Instead, their faith should be in believing that God can—and *will*—do what *He* said that He would do.

The modern approach to faith lacks confidence in God. True faith is confidence that God is faithful. If we believe that, we will more eagerly seek to know what His promises are and what He said that He would or would not do concerning them.

Jesus taught that faith is not rooted in the ability of the individual but rather the ability of God. We should ask, "What did God say about it?" Then be certain that God will do what He said. Once that principle is applied, it will produce the manifestation of what is "hoped for." Every believer must have confident assurance that God is always faithful to His promises.

Belief, the Foundation to Faith in God

After leaving Bethany, Jesus became hungry and, seeing a fig tree in the distance having an abundance of leaves, went to the tree, scoured it for figs, but found none. It wasn't time for the tree to bear fruit, so there wasn't any.

Jesus then spoke to the tree, declaring that no one would eat fruit from it ever again. His disciples heard what He spoke to the tree. The next morning, seeing how quickly the tree had withered away, His disciples were amazed. Responding to their inquiry, Jesus told them that for such things to be done, they must have faith in God. He told them that anytime they prayed and believed God, they would receive the things they asked (Mark 11:22–24).

It is our confident belief in God, His Word, and His works that serve as the foundation for our faith in God. God cannot be separated from His Word, His Spirit, or His works.

Every challenge of the devil is focused and directed toward undermining our faith in God. Why? It's because the devil knows that if he can get believers to lose faith in God, everything in their lives will be downhill from there.

The key to our success and all that we do is dependent upon one thing: having faith in God. If undermining our faith in God is the devil's focus, our focus should be on increasing our faith in God. Every believer should be committed to holding onto and growing in their confidence in God. "Faith in God" will make doing so possible.

Three Things to Know about Faith in God

Every believer should remember the following three things about faith in God; learn and write them on the table of your heart:

1. *Faith in God is trust in God. Faith in God is developed through confident trust in God. Every believer must grow to the point where they have total confidence that God will do what He said He would do. Such confidence can only come from an abiding trust in God.*

2. *Faith in God grows as our relationship with God grows. Trust in God results from a personal, intimate relationship with God. Growth in your relationship with God will increase your faith in God. Time spent with those in*

any relationship reveals character and will increase or decrease trust between the ones in the relationship. Getting to know God better will reveal His character, which should increase faith in God.

3. *Faith in God is confidence in God, not self-confidence. Faith in God is sustained by realizing that your confidence and abilities rest in God and* His *abilities. Our ability to do and accomplish should be squarely rooted in confidence in God and who we are in Him. What we do as believers is a result of Him working in and expressing Himself through us.*

A Closer Look into "Having Faith in God"

Our faith in God is not only a reflection of our relationship with God; it's a reflection of our confidence in Him. It's through confidence in God that we realize the things we are hoping for. I know that many of us believe that faith is not doubting, a type of inner confidence, but it isn't. The confidence of faith is really an attribute resulting from our belief and trust. That's why confidence is always present with faith. Instead of focusing on confidence, we should focus on what we believe and whom we trust.

Believers often try to have the confidence to show that they have faith when they really should be working on the depth of their trust in God. Increasing trust will increase belief, which will increase faith, which will then produce that confident feeling they seek.

Remember the following:

a. Faith in God is the means by which we access God's will for our lives.

b. Faith in God is the catalyst by which our confidence is activated.

c. Faith in God gives us confidence to do what we must and desire.

d. Faith in God fosters courage to face significant challenges and seemingly insurmountable odds.

I must get a little heady here to convey a few insights into what Jesus said when He directed His disciples to "have faith in God." To do that, we'll look at each word in the original Greek text: "have" "faith" "in" God (Mark 11:22).

Have: "Have" in the original Greek is *echo (ekh'-o)*, a primary verb; it is always active. It means "to hold, keep, possessed with" (Strong's Concordance). It is the ability to hold, to maintain continuity, relation, or condition (Strong's Concordance). Jesus is saying, "Acquire, hold onto, and keep your trust in God."

Additionally, Jesus' use of the word "have" includes the alternate form of the Greek word *scheo (skheh'-o)*: "*that which is* of necessity, sick, diseased, fear, uncircumcised, etc." This definition conveys the idea that no matter the state of one's life, no matter what the person may be going through, they can and should "have faith in God." The individual makes the choice.

Faith: "Faith" in the Greek text is *pistis* (pis'-tis), "persuasion," i.e., "credence": "*belief in or acceptance of something as true*" (Strong's Concordance). The person of faith must believe that

God is honest. They must believe that God is truth. Faith becomes impossible without those two components. God is what truth is. That means that He is the embodiment of honesty.

In: The word "in" represents the location and placement of faith. Every person of faith should place their faith squarely *in* God.

By using the word "in," Jesus indicated that believers must allow their confidence to be encapsulated by trust in God. Like a person "in" the house or "in" the car is encapsulated by the house or car, so should our faith be encapsulated with trust in God. Unyielding trust in God will prevent one from becoming wavery-minded.

The word "in" is also a preposition that lets us know upon whom our faith rests: upon God. With rare exceptions, faith should not depend exclusively on one's self or one's own personal abilities or inabilities. Faith should not be placed in what seems to be the enormity of the problem. Believing that an obstacle can't be overcome is paramount to having faith in the obstacle or faith that the obstacle can't be overcome. The believer's faith should only be "in" God.

God: The key to Jesus' instruction was where our faith should be directed. The fact of the matter is that you, me, and everyone else have faith. The question is where that faith is directed. Jesus said, "Direct it to God." But why? Consider the following:

1. *Agreement.* Underlying all faith is an agreement between the one having the faith and in whom or what the one having the faith places their faith. Everything is established through agreement. Our first choice when standing in faith is who or what we will move into

agreement with. That one thing will determine the course and outcome of every situation or circumstance. Jesus is saying, "Move into agreement with God." Consider Matthew 18:19 (KJV), "*...if two of you shall agree on earth as touching any thing that they shall ask, it shall be done for them of my Father which is in heaven.*" When walking in faith, enter into agreement with God first, then reject anyone or anything that conflicts with that agreement.

2. *Creation.* God is the Creator. It's not that God creates; it's that God is the embodiment of creation. When faith is needed, there is something needed that doesn't exist. Hebrews 11:1 (KJV), "*...faith is the substance of things hoped for, the evidence of things not seen.*" If you are hoping for it, it doesn't exist, or it isn't where it needs to be. An act of creation is required, and God is what creation is. Who better to have faith in?

3. As an aside, God poured His creative ability into us; moving into agreement with Him cemented and unleashed that ability, enabling us to do what we must, to realize the things hoped for.

4. *Life.* What do you want to live or give life to? John 1:3–4 (KJV) says, *"All things were made by him; and without him was not any thing made that was made. In him was life; and the life was the light of men."* God not only made everything; He is the maker of everything. He is life. That means that God is life itself. He is what life is. He is also the giver of life. When what we need, want, or desire doesn't exist, it not only has to be created, it must be brought to life. That is done by and in God

through us. We initiate that process through our faith in God.

No matter who you are, you must be fully persuaded and committed to God. You must have unwavering trust in Him. You must also remain focused, no matter the distraction. You must also aggressively and intelligently respond to each challenge you face, doing so tenaciously. You must never give up, even when it seems hopeless. It is often in times of hopelessness that we can most clearly see the hand of God working in our lives.

Lastly, become and remain humble. No matter what happens, remain reflexively, responsive, and obedient to God. Be obedient to every word of instruction that God gives. True humility will always respond reflexively, obediently to the one that is trusted. The truly humble will always respond reflexively to God and His instructions. Why? Because the humility of faith is rooted in trust, and we don't usually resist or doubt that in which we trust.

CHAPTER 4:

TRUST IN GOD

Everyone who truly believes in God must come to the place where they know that faith and trust in God are inseparable. One cannot have faith in God without trusting God.

Trust in God depends upon trusting God. Do you really trust God? Do you take Him at His word? If you do not trust God, you will struggle in your faith and life. This trust is not simply an awareness that God is real and can do anything, but rather that God is real and will do *your* thing. This assumes, however, that your thing isn't in opposition to His will, plan, and purpose.

True faith is not being confident that *you* can do enough or believe enough to manifest what you are hoping for, but rather having trust in God that God will do *what He said* about what you are hoping for. That means trusting that God will do exactly what He said He would do. Every believer must conclude that God is always worthy of our trust. We must always defer to His will in every situation and circumstance.

Always be mindful of the following:

1. Faith is confidence in God and being confident that God will do what He said He would do. Be aware, however,

that our struggle in believing God is usually not a matter of whether or not God can but whether or not He will. So, rather than focusing on when and if you are going to get what you want, always ask yourself what God said about what you want. Make sure that what you desire and/or are asking is in line with God's will, plan, and purpose for your life and others. To do that, you have to make sure that your heart is in the right place. That will mean that your motives are selfless and in harmony with God's Word.

2. You can be confident that God will always do what He said He would do. You can be certain of the fact that God cannot and will not lie. Let that be your blessed assurance.

3. Faith is trusting that God has or will equip and enable you to do what He has or is directing you to do. God never directs us to do anything and then leaves it up to us to equip ourselves. God always gives or otherwise provides the resources necessary to succeed.

Measuring Your Trust in God

Trust in God can be measured by the depth of our commitment and obedience to Him. Three of the most common reasons for disobedience to God are ignorance, rebellion, and lack of trust. If we trust God, we will be committed and obedient to Him. A victorious Christian life depends upon total, absolute trust in God; there is no way around that.

Again, how much do you trust God the person? Can you, in your heart and mind, bridge the gap between trusting God the Creator and God the person? We tend to view God as a self-existent thing, but if we begin to see Him as an individual, our approach to him will change, and so will our relationship with Him. I do not intend to get hung up on this nuance, but it is important to trust the person that is God and not the thing we perceive Him to be.

Merely saying that you trust God is too general, subjective, indirect, and impersonal. It's also too nondescript. Saying "I trust God" doesn't complete the circle of trust. It does not close the relational gap that trust creates. It also lacks the emotional attachment needed to solidify the commitment that trusting an individual brings.

When we truly trust God the person, our trust is directed to Him personally and not to God the placeholder. It is vitally important that our trust be placed in the individual who is God. Doing so will change the very dynamics of your faith. Trusting God the person is necessary to facilitate faith in God.

Job saw this and went from sackcloth and ashes to receiving double for his troubles. One of my favorite verses of Scripture is Job 42:5. Job and his friend spent extensive time verbally sparring and finger-pointing. Everyone used their view of God to stake out positions.

After the exchange of conversation between Job and his friends had gone on at length, God stepped in, speaking out of the whirlwind. When Job heard God speak and saw His presence in the whirlwind, Job said, in essence, "I heard about You, but now I see You with my own eyes." That shift in awareness not only changed Job's relationship with God but also changed his life. Such a shift will also change your life and your faith. Such a transition can only take place through the kind of personal relationship that comes through spending time in the presence of God.

We all come to some level of faith in God through what we hear about Him. Remember Romans 10:17 (KJV), *"So then faith cometh by hearing..."* Hearsay is okay to initiate a relationship, but unless there is some level of personal involvement, that relationship will not be strengthened. The same is true with our relationship with God. As we get to know God personally, our relationship with God becomes closer, deeper, and stronger, and so does our faith.

Simply put, no one can have a personal relationship with God when that relationship is filtered only through others. It is difficult to develop true faith in God through a filtered relationship with God. Every believer must have a one-on-one, personal, intimate relationship with God that is not dependent upon anyone or anything else but God.

Never be satisfied with being a hear-say Christian. Doing so will prevent you from developing a personal, intimate relationship with God, making it near impossible to truly trust God. Remember faith in God is developed through having a personal, intimate relationship with God. Such a relationship will always yield strong, unwavering trust in God.

Growing Your Trust in God

Hopefully, I have established that trusting God is vitally important to faith and to every believer's walk in Christ. So how do we build and maintain our trust in God the person? There are at least four things that must be done to build trust in God the person:

1. *You must spend time with Him...* The Lord must become our priority. Spending time with God is the only way anyone can truly get to know God. Spending time with God starts by spending time reading His Word. Not as a

novel but as a way of gaining insight into God the person, learning His thoughts, and the way He thinks. Spending time with God also requires spending time in His presence and in worship and fellowship with the brethren. This type of worship and fellowship is not religious but relational.

2. *Recognize and take notice consistently* of what God is doing and has done in your life and in the life of others.

3. *Give God credit* for what He has done and is doing. Doing so will help you to grow in confidence for what He can and will do in your life and in the earth.

4. *Give God a chance.* You will never build the confidence in God that you need if you do not allow Him to show Himself strong in your life. It comes down to control and risk. If you stay at the helm of your life, you will never move into the place that God intends for you to be. If you don't risk doing things God's way, you will never get the outcomes for your life that He has ordained.

The prophet Samuel admonished King Saul, saying, *"...to obey is better than sacrifice, and to listen than the fat of rams"* (1 Samuel 15:22, ESV). Too often, we unnecessarily pay more for life's experiences than we should. There are also those times when we pay life's price for things that we shouldn't pay for at all. We do so because we choose to do things our way and not God's. That is rebellion. Rebellion is much more than disobedience and lack of submission; it is also a displacement of trust.

One day my eventual stepdad was teaching me to drive. We were headed back home when we came to a place where there was a tree in the center of the road. We both saw the tree ahead, but his approach to navigating around the tree was different from mine.

In my mind, I was going to begin my turn as I came close to the tree, then follow the contour of the road around the tree. In the mind of the more experienced driver to my right, one doesn't allow himself to get that close to the tree before beginning his turn. So he grabbed the steering wheel, turned the vehicle away from the tree, and with a scolding, relieved me of my driving experience.

My driving experience may not be the perfect example of what I'm about to say, but I'm certain you will see the correlation. We will never develop the trust that is needed for great faith when we constantly remove God's hands from the steering wheel of our life. We grab the steering wheel when we don't trust the driver. When we don't trust the driver, we take control, try to control, or continually wish we were in control. In each instance, there is no room for trust, so trust is displaced.

It comes down to control. Who's in control often comes down to trust. In reality, we trust ourselves and others more than we trust God. Will you or God be in control? It's foolish to be at the wheel when you don't know where to go and will not listen to the instructions that will get you there. Unfortunately, and too often, that is what we do. Such actions diminish trust and will not develop it.

Take a chance on giving God the control of your life. Doing so will not only grow your trust in God; it will grow your faith in God. To have great faith in God, you must have great trust in God. That's truly the only way to have faith in God. Your faith will always be in direct relation and proportion to your trust.

Action Plan 1: Believe in God

But without faith it is impossible to please him: for he that cometh to God must believe that he is, and that he is a rewarder of them that diligently seek him.
Hebrews 11:6 (KJV)

In the above verse, the word "believe" in the original Greek is *pisteuo* (pist-yoo'-o), meaning to "have faith (in, upon, or with respect to, a person or thing)," i.e., "credit," "to commit (to trust), put in trust with" (Strong's Concordance).

Normally, when we are facing our mountains, we are facing something that is (in the natural) bigger than we are and that we cannot handle. That is just one reason why faith in God is important. If we, in our strength and ability, could move our mountain, the mountain would not be there. It would not because we would not allow it to be. We would have gotten it out of the way long before it became a problem, or at least not long thereafter.

There will come a time in each of our lives when we will have to conquer something bigger, stronger, and more formidable than we are individually. When that time comes, we must first realize that that thing is bigger than we are only when confronting it in our strength alone.

Once we become one with Christ, we become much bigger and greater than anything that we can possibly face. That's because we are not confronting it alone but with, in, and through Jesus Christ. That is what faith in God is about. Our entering into oneness with Christ and, through Him, oneness with God.

To have "faith in God," we must first believe that God is, that He is real, alive, present, able, that He is aware, etc.

Secondly, we must believe that God will give us (in accord with His will) what we are seeking. The important thing is that we must believe in God's integrity. Ask yourself, "Is God a person of integrity, and will God do what He says?" If the answer is a firm yes and then comes Hades or high water, hold to that. Hold on to your faith in God.

"And this is the confidence that we have "in him, that, if we ask anything according "to his will, he heareth us." First John 5:14 (KJV)

The third thing that is unique to people of great faith *is their unwavering, unshakable, undeniable trust in God.* Such trust is a result of their oneness with God. You, too, can know that your faith is where it needs to be when you have unwavering, unshakable, undeniable trust in God. It is at that point that you can be assured that you have faith in God.

Remember, that little word "in" is the key to having faith in God. Again, the word "in" is a preposition that expresses the relation between what came before it and what follows it. It illustrates the location and position of faith. Never forget that your trust and confidence must reside squarely in God. Not in what He can or will do but in Him as a person. Your confidence in what He can or will do is a byproduct of your confidence in Him individually.

Having faith in God means that you realize that your ability to accomplish is because of Him. It means that you are in Him, doing what you do through Him while He is working and expressing Himself through you. Your confidence in God must be the foundation upon which your confidence lies, no matter what you may be trying to achieve.

"I can do all things through Christ which strengtheneth me."Philippians 4:13 (KJV)

To-do list:

- *Always* know (believe) that God is.
- *Always* believe that God will.
- *Always* trust God.

Trust in God will facilitate oneness with God. Oneness is key to faith in God. No matter how things may look, trust Him, even if it kills you to do so. If you do, you can truly declare with certainty that you "have faith in God."

Thought to Remember

True faith is not self-confidence
but being confident in God.

Faith Is Focused

...he that wavereth is like a wave of the
sea driven with the wind and tossed.
A double minded man is
unstable in all his ways. James 1:6, 8 (KJV)

CHAPTER 5:

FAITH IS ALWAYS FOCUSED

Focused. True faith is always focused. This portion of *Faith Made Easy* will be a little heady and technical, but it is necessary to fully understand why being focused is so important to faith.

To become faith-focused, one must achieve a oneness that yields clarity, clarity of thought, ideas, interest, activity, etc. All those things must become perfectly aligned and in complete agreement in the heart and mind in such a way as to produce clarity and certainty. Ideas, thoughts, desires, things being said or done must agree with each other and with the objective that is trying to be reached.

When a person is faith-focused, there is no uncertainty, no waviness, ambiguity, or double-mindedness. A faith-focused person has clarity of mind, thought, ideas, attention, and emotion. Their heart, soul, and mind are all in agreement; they must be at one. The faith-focused person is not swayed by the circumstances or divergent ideas.

Being faith-focused directs one's attention, interest, and activity to a specific objective. Focus creates the synergy of faith, a point in which everything necessary to manifest the thing being "hoped for" comes together. Once that happens, the manifestation of the thing being "hoped for" is assured.

At the center of all faith is the thing hoped for. Everything that takes place in the heart and mind of the believer, from the inception of that hope to the full manifestation, is directed and geared to that one thing. It is important, however, to realize that there are things that must take place in both the natural and spiritual realms before the manifestation takes place.

Hope (for the thing) is like a magnet that draws together as needed the things that will establish the manifestation. Losing hope will cause the loss of focus, and the loss of focus will diminish faith. This is why focus is so important to faith. The sharper and clearer the focus, the stronger the draw and the quicker the manifestation of the thing being hoped for. Losing focus could be the main reason so many believers lose faith.

To maintain focus, we must reject each thing said, whatever is done, and every thought, idea, or desire that does not agree with the thing hoped for.

However, this rejection must be of and by the Holy Spirit, not the flesh. The flesh will always seek to preserve itself and do so with little to no consideration of the consequence of its actions. The Holy Spirit will always consider the ways and mind of God to establish the will of God. Doing so always results in outcomes that are pleasing to God, and that is good for the person of faith and others.

It is important to understand that the focus of faith is not merely being confident; it is not positive thinking; it is not mind over matter or not being distracted. The focus of faith is directing and aligning events, situations, attention, interest, desires, etc., to a specific objective, the thing being hoped for, and doing so in accordance with God's will.

Remember true focus is reaching the point in which the believer becomes one with God (concerning the thing being hoped for). If focus is lost, faith fails. That is what happened with Peter in Matthew 14:24–32.

Losing Focus

Matthew tells the story of Jesus walking on water to the boat in which were His disciples. At the time, the boat was being tossed to and fro by winds and waves. The disciples, not knowing it was Jesus walking on water, thought they were seeing a ghost. As a result, they began to cry out in fear. Jesus calmed them by saying, "Be of good cheer; it is I; be not afraid."

Peter replied to Jesus, "If it is You, let me come to You on the water." Jesus answered, "Come." Peter, almost without thinking, got out of the boat and began walking on water toward Jesus.

The winds were blowing, the waves choppy, but Peter, not paying attention to any of those things, focused only on going to Jesus. Peter entered into a place of oneness with Jesus. Once Peter came into oneness (not just acceptance) with what Jesus said, he also entered into oneness with Jesus Himself. As a result, Peter walked on water just as Jesus was walking on water. They were at one.

Something happened, however, between Peter's getting out of the boat and reaching Jesus, he lost focus. Peter lost his focus on Jesus, what Jesus said, and the thing he hoped for. As Peter lost focus, he lost hope; as he lost hope, he lost faith and progressively began to sink. Peter redirected his attention away from Jesus and what Jesus told him to do onto the winds and waves. As he did, he began to sink and cried out for Jesus. Reaching down, Jesus grabbed Peter and kept him from drowning. Afterward, they both returned to the boat. I doubt that Jesus carried Peter to the boat. My guess is that Peter re-focused and walked back.

We see this example of what can happen when we lose focus. Peter was getting the thing he was hoping for until he looked at the circumstances.

Focusing on those circumstances, Peter lost focus on Jesus and what Jesus said, causing him to lose faith while gaining faith in the circumstances.

Too often, we, like Peter, take our eyes off Jesus and the reason we were trusting Him and become distracted by the various things that comprise our circumstances. Doing so will always cause us to lose focus and begin to doubt. When that happens, we lose faith.

Focus brings clarity; clarity helps us to see; seeing helps us to embrace, and when we embrace the Lord, we will always be filled with confidence in Him. That confidence will bring us to the place where we will not only believe *in* the Lord but *believe* the Lord. It's at that point we begin to have faith in God.

Jesus is the reason believers have true faith. Their belief is founded upon what He said, what He has done, and what He is doing. Never allow the circumstances to compete in your mind with what Jesus said. Always let God's word settle it for you. Let His word be the final word. It will take some practice, but if you train yourself to stay focused on His word and not allow yourself to be swayed by the circumstances, your faith will not fail.

When you find yourself becoming distracted by the circumstances, do what 2 Corinthians 10:5 (KJV) instructs, "*Casting down imaginations, and every high thing that exalteth itself against the knowledge of God, and bringing into captivity every thought to the obedience of Christ.*"

Distractions are the enemy's efforts to get you to redirect your focus from the Lord, His Word, and the thing that you are hoping for. That is where the real battle of faith lies, but it is a battle that you can and must win. You must, however, respond in accordance with God's word; your doing so is the key to your victory.

You literally have to throw down, pull down, or in whatever way, bring down every single thought, reason, reasoning, conclusion, etc., that are contrary to your commitment and focus on the Lord, His Word, and the thing that you are hoping for. Then, you must hold your own mind together. You must not allow events to redirect your focus away from what God said. You must also allow the word to bring and keep you in focus. Get started by hearing, reading, and learning God's Word and by meditating on it.

The goal is to become one with God through moving in agreement with His Word. Then, use God's Word as a means to stay focused. Do that by making sure that you believe and do only what God's Word says. Then remain in agreement with His Word. Don't reject it. Doing those few things will keep you in agreement with God and keep you in true focus.

Not losing focus is the difference between walking on water and sinking into it. It is also the difference between having a promise and possessing the promise. Staying focused is a must if you are going to have faith in God.

Maintaining Focus

In Mark chapter 5, verses 22–43, Jairus came to Jesus, asking Him to heal his daughter, who was close to death. Before they arrived at Jairus' house, messengers arrived with bad news; his daughter had died. As soon as Jesus heard those words, He told Jairus, "Be not afraid, only believe." Jesus was telling Jairus (in essence) not to lose focus. He didn't, and his daughter was raised up.

Jesus knew that if Jairus began to focus on the circumstances, he would believe the circumstances and thereby establish them. Once Jairus heard the report that his daughter had died, he had to make a choice, believe the report of the messengers or believe Jesus. How and what Jairus believed was going to determine whether his daughter was sleeping or dead.

Jairus' faith was in Jesus, so he kept his focus on what Jesus said, "…only believe." He did just that, and his daughter lived and was completely healed. Jairus' acceptance of what Jesus said was an automatic rejection of the report given by the messengers that his daughter had already died.

We see here a contrast of focus between Peter and Jairus; one, as with Peter, losing focus; the other, as with Jairus, maintaining focus. One yielded success; the other near failure. As with Peter and Jairus, when we ask and believe the Lord for the things we hope for, our ability to remain focused is key to receiving them.

Always be aware that the key to acquiring and maintaining focus is believing, first, in God, and secondly, that God will bring you into possession of the thing you are hoping for. Remember also that focus doesn't necessarily stop the winds or the waves, nor does focus always prevent negative outcomes. It does, however, help us to realize and accomplish that for which we are believing the Lord.

If you want to know if you or anyone else is walking in faith, simply ask if you or they are still focused. Not focused on any old thing but focused on God. Why? Because your faith must be in

Him and on the thing or things for which you are hoping.

Not having the things being "hoped for" is why you are where you are in the first place. If you lose sight of what you are hoping for, you will lose purpose, and then you will lose motivation. If that happens, failure is all but assured. If you maintain focus, you can maintain your faith in God, all but assuring that you will receive the thing for which you are hoping.

A Perspective on Focusing Your Faith

Thus far, we have discussed focusing on two things: (1) focus on the thing being "hoped for" and (2) focus on God.

I don't want to muddy the waters too much, but to reach the point of true focus, the focus on the thing being hoped for and the focus on God must merge. Yes, focusing on God and the thing you are hoping for must become one. So how do we do that? We focus our attention on God without displacing our desire for the thing being hoped for. That is done by trusting God for the thing being hoped for. We can see how this works by looking at the relationship between God and Abraham.

As believers, we must always remember that faith in God is trust in God, and trust in God depends upon trusting God. If we do not trust God, we will struggle in our faith and, therefore, in our lives. A victorious Christian life depends upon total and absolute trust in God. Again, we see that level of trust consistently in Abraham's life.

The story begins in Genesis chapter 12, when at seventy-five years old, the Lord spoke to Abram (Abraham's name at the time), instructing him to leave his relatives. If he did, the Lord told him that He would create from him a great nation, bless him, and make his name great.

Today we can look back and see that God kept His promise to Abram. Now, let's fast forward twenty-five years. Abraham, now a hundred years old, has two children, Ishmael, his oldest, approximately thirteen years old, and Isaac, his youngest. Isaac, at the time, was just weaned. Ishmael began mocking his little brother, infuriating Sarah, Isaac's mother. Sarah then insisted to Abraham that he send both Ishmael and his mother, Hagar, away.

The demand grieved Abraham. However, God encouraged him and instructed him to do what his wife was insisting, assuring him that He would take care of Ishmael. God also told Abraham that the covenant would be established through Isaac. This conversation with God was key to Abraham's faith and our destiny.

Sometime later (some believe Isaac was in his teens or older), God directs Abraham to offer Isaac as a sacrifice to Him. Abraham didn't hesitate and would have done so if God hadn't stopped him.

Why would Abraham not hesitate to offer the son he loved as a sacrifice to God? The answer: his faith in God. The event unfolds in Genesis chapter 22, but Hebrews 11:17–19 gives us a few insights into Abraham's thinking.

"By faith Abraham, when he was tried, offered up Isaac: and he that had received the promises offered up his only begotten son." Hebrews 11:17 (KJV)

"Of whom it was said, That in Isaac shall thy seed be called." Hebrews 11:18 (KJV),

"Accounting that God was able to raise him up, even from the dead; from whence also he received him in a figure." Hebrews 11:19 (KJV)

Abraham believed God. As a result, he believed that God would raise Isaac from the dead. Abraham didn't lose sight or focus on the thing he hoped for; he maintained that focus by focusing on God. He knew that God would keep His word; therefore, he knew that to do so, God would even reverse death.

To maintain the focus of faith, you must stay centered upon God and what He says. To do that, you must trust Him. Trusting God includes submitting to God's will. Trust yields submission; therefore, the thing you're hoping for will be in agreement with God's will.

Secondly, we must decide upon the thing we are hoping for. Know what you want, know God's promise concerning it, and don't vacillate. Thirdly, believe God for the outcome. If you are not confident that God can and will, you will not believe Him for your desired outcome. Such belief and confidence start with believing God's word.

Lastly, focus on God, not the circumstances, and don't focus on whether or not you will lose the thing you are hoping for or whether or not you will fail or suffer loss. Keep your focus on God. You must get to the place where if God said it, for you, it's settled.

Focusing on God means that you believe God to keep and provide for you. Focusing on God means that you believe God will do what He promised. Focusing on God means that you accept, believe, and apply Numbers 23:19 (KJV), "*God is not a man, that he should lie; neither the son of man, that he should repent: hath he said, and shall he not do it? or hath he spoken, and shall he not make it good?*"

Action Plan 2:
Focus On What God Said about It

"Only be thou strong and very courageous, that thou mayest observe to do according to all the law, which Moses my servant commanded thee: turn not from it to the right hand or to the left, that thou mayest prosper whithersoever thou goest." Joshua 1:7 (KJV)

When going through anything, ask yourself:

(1) What did God say about it?

(2) What did God say that He would do about it?

(3) What did God tell *you* to do about it?

(4) What are you doing about it?

If your answers to those questions are in the affirmative, then rest assured that you are within God's will, and God always establishes His will.

Faith Is Always Aggressive

"Fight the good fight of faith,
lay hold on eternal life, whereunto
"thou art also called..." First Timothy 6:12 (KJV)

CHAPTER 6:

THE AGGRESSIVENESS OF FAITH

Faith is always aggressive, but the aggressiveness of faith is not carnal aggression. Carnal aggression exhibits some level of hostility, violent behavior or attitudes toward others, and a readiness to attack or confront. Carnal aggression strives to accomplish self-will, while the aggressiveness of faith seeks to align with God to accomplish His will. The natural man's carnal nature uses aggression to establish its own will.

Those dependent upon their carnal nature use aggressiveness to fulfill their will, regardless of what the will of God might be. Not so among believers. Those who are led by the Spirit of God continually pursue the will of God. They, from the heart, passionately seek to establish God's will in all that they say and do.

The aggressiveness of faith always seeks to establish and maintain God's will. Aggressive faith will and should consistently manifest itself in at least four areas in the life of every believer:

1. in a willingness to engage with confidence in the activities necessary to establish the will, plan, and purpose of God;

2. in confidence that God will act to establish His will;

3. in God-given confidence to do what's needed to accomplish needed victories—such victories will always come through God working in and through the believer's life and the lives of others; and

4. in being determined and willing, through God, to challenge confidently, energetically, passionately, and forcefully that which challenges the believer's confidence in God.

The aggressiveness of faith will also be used by the believer to:

1. Establish the will, plan, and purpose of God.

2. Allow God to act through them to establish His perfect and divine will.

3. Have the willingness, through God, to challenge that which challenges them, but do so in harmony with God's will.

Faith is always aggressive. The aggressiveness of faith is confrontational tenaciousness and passionate commitment to our relationship with our heavenly Father. It is the fight that is needed when the enemy attacks and seeks to get us to turn away from God, His promises, and the thing or things "we are hoping for."

The aggressiveness of faith is the passionate, spirited, assertive resistance brought to bear while seeking to adhere to or establish the will, plan, and purpose of God.

The aggressiveness of faith is also that which transforms mere endurance into energetic, engaging tenacity. It is the aggressiveness of faith that adds energy and fight to faith and becomes the motivation to press forward, even when things seem to be hopeless.

The Two Fights of Faith

There will always be two objectives of the devil any time we're standing in faith. The first is to prevent the will, plan, and purpose of God from being established, and the second is to undermine confidence in God.

The objective for the believer should be to do one thing: believe God. Most, if not all, of the believer's efforts should be focused right there. Believing God is what faith in God is all about. In fact, believing God *is* faith in God. The believer's attention and efforts should not be to "have faith" for a job or a car or this or that but to have faith in God. Simply believe God. As a believer in the one and only true and living God, everything the enemy does is done to get you to question God. If he succeeds, you will begin to doubt God, and from there, the battle will be all but over.

In 1 Timothy 6:12 (ESV), believers are instructed to "*Fight the good fight of faith.*" The first use of the word "fight" in the verse means "to contend with an adversary, to labor fervently, strive to accomplish, etc."

There will come those times in the life of every believer when they will have to fight while standing in faith. They will have to engage in the struggles and face the challenges that are enviably necessary to accomplish or acquire the thing for which they are hoping. There will also come those times when they will have to face their adversaries directly. In either event, they must maintain their faith in God.

There will also come those times when believers will find it necessary to face the inevitable challenges of accomplishments. No matter the challenge, no matter the opposition, there will be one thing that will be constant: the challenge to our faith in God.

The question will be asked in one way or another: Will God do what He said? Will you, the believer, remain faithful to God, even if things do not turn out as expected? The question for each of us is: Will we have and hold on to our faith *in* God? Will we "*Fight the good fight of faith*"?

The first "fight" of faith in 1 Timothy 6:12 also means to stand in firm, unfaltering, unfailing opposition to the enemy while at the same time being intransigently committed to God, even to death. If we do this as a believer, we can rest assured that we are fighting the good fight of faith each time we face opposition.

The second "fight" in the "good fight of faith" is to stand in total and complete commitment and allegiance to God. There will be those times when each of us must stand unflinchingly in our commitment and allegiance to God. We must do so even when it seems that all hope has been lost. Shadrach, Meshach, and Abednego may have felt that way when they were cast into a furnace that was so hot it glowed. Their story unfolds in Daniel chapter 3 with a defining moment of faith in God.

King Nebuchadnezzar made an image of gold and decreed that everyone must bow down and worship the image upon hearing the instruments announcing that they and others do so. Shadrach, Meshach, and Abednego, without hesitation, resolved in their hearts that they would not. For them to do so would violate the laws of the true and living God.

The king declared that if they did not bow before the idol, they would be cast into a furnace and burnt alive. Their reply is recorded in verses 17 and 18 (ESV), *"If this be so, our God whom we serve is able to deliver us from the burning fiery furnace, and he will deliver us out of your hand, O king. But if not, be it known to you, O king, that we will not serve your gods or worship the golden image that you have set up."* Now that is a perfect example of the aggressiveness of faith, and it is an unmitigated display of faith in God.

It is important to remember that without fail, at the root of every challenge of the enemy is his goal to get the believer to reject God. This was true with Adam and Eve; it was true with Job, and it was true with Shadrach, Meshach, and Abednego; it is also his goal today for every believer. Shadrach, Meshach, and Abednego stood with God, placing them at odds with King Nebuchadnezzar.

Because of their defiant commitment to God, those three young men were immediately tied up, fully dressed, hats and all, then cast into the furnace. The furnace was so hot that not only did it glow red hot, the heat was so intense that the men throwing them in were engulfed by the flames and immediately killed while doing so.

Being tied, Shadrach, Meshach, and Abednego fell down in the furnace, got up, and began praising God with an angel in the furnace. The king, with amazement, saw that not only were they not consumed by the flames, he saw what he concluded was an angel from God in the furnace with them. The king called them out, praised God himself, and issued another decree that anyone that did not respect Shadrach, Meshach, and Abednego or their God would be destroyed along with their family.

Like Shadrach, Meshach, and Abednego, people of faith never wavered in their commitment to God. That is the evidence of their faith, and that is why aggressiveness in faith is so important.

Too often, we become so focused on getting what we want that we fail to realize the real battle of faith is in our relationship and commitment to God. If we lose that, we lose everything. Is getting what you want worth losing your relationship with your heavenly

Father? I say not. Nothing is worth losing our relationship with God. That is why faith in God must and will always be aggressive. It will consistently display the passionate commitment that says, "I will die before I deny Him or disbelieve Him or dishonor Him."

True faith in God will always place God's will over self-will. Faith in God aggressively seeks to preserve, restore (if necessary), and maintain one's relationship with God. True faith in God will never allow one to disbelieve God. While having faith in God, we will not always know the outcome, but we will know that we will remain faithful to him, just as He is faithful to us. We'll do so regardless of the outcome.

The aggressiveness of faith considers who you are in God, then, with confidence, determines a course of action (works) to put forth that will lead to the accomplishing of the will, plan, and purpose of God, which will include the things being hoped for.

On one hand, the aggressiveness of faith brings to bear the determination, energy, and forcefulness necessary to receive, accomplish, or possess the things "hoped for," while on the other hand, it ensures that we vigorously establish, keep, and maintain our place and position in God. The aggressiveness of faith is key to keeping us in the center of God's will and fighting to do so or die trying.

There are times when we need the audaciousness (bold risk-taking) of aggressiveness in order to receive the things that we are hoping for. Without it, our faith is all but sure to falter when confronted by the challenges of the enemy.

In today's societies, aggression is too often frowned upon, primarily because of its carnal misuse. That's unfortunate for us as believers because we have a tendency to display confidence primarily when the challenges are well within the scope of our abilities, but what about those challenges that are bigger or greater than we are?

What happens when one thing that confronts us becomes multiple things that are confronting us? What do we do when we see and know that our strength, abilities, contacts, and ability to maneuver will not get us out of or away from what challenges us? That, my dear child of God, is when you must bring to bear the aggressiveness of faith. If you don't have it, it will only be by God's grace that you will not be defeated.

Always remember this: We only feel challenged when we perceive that our strengths and abilities are or will be insufficient to meet the challenge being faced. An example can be seen in 1 Samuel chapter 17. Be sure to read the full text to see the events surrounding the story of David and Goliath.

David, the skinny little shepherd boy, and the giant of a man, the Philistines champion Goliath, the nine-foot-nine-tall man of war. The sequence of events unfolds while David was at home tending his father Jessie's sheep. Jessie sent David to deliver food to his brothers and to pay their taxes to King Saul.

When David arrived at the location of the battle, "*...the Philistines stood on a mountain on the one side, and Israel stood on a mountain on the other side: and there was a valley between them*" (1 Samuel 17:3, KJV).

Upon arriving at the battle sight, David heard Goliath shouting obscenities against Israel and God. Goliath also put forth a challenge to Israel, saying, *"And the Philistine said, I defy the armies of Israel this day; give me a man, that we may fight together. When Saul and all Israel heard those words of the Philistine, they were dismayed, and greatly afraid"* (1 Samuel 17:10–11, KJV).

So what do you do when your challenges are bigger, greater, and in this case, worse than you are? When the king and his army heard the dare and saw what they had to overcome to meet the challenge, they were petrified. David had far less going for him with no combat abilities or experience, but his response was, in essence, "Let me at him!"

As an aside, always remember: It is likely that there will be a great obstacle that will stand between you and your place of destiny. Never be afraid of the challenge. Usually, there will be positioning and reward after the defeat of the challenge. So don't be afraid of the things others run away from. Always see the possible in what others call impossible. Always remember that you can do all things through Christ who strengthens you (Philippians 4:13). When everyone is running, consider that as God clearing the stage for you to perform and accomplish His will. Make sure, however, that you are led by God when doing so.

David, in verse 26 (KJV), said, *"...What shall be done to the man that killeth this Philistine, and taketh away the reproach from Israel? for who is this uncircumcised Philistine, that he should defy the armies of the living God?"*

David's response was rooted in the aggressiveness that can only come from having faith in God. What we saw in David when he confronted Goliath is the same thing that must be in us when challenged by our giants. We must have the aggressiveness of faith.

The aggressiveness of faith is not arrogance; it's not condescension; it's not rooted in one's own abilities. Such faith is rooted in the abilities of God. As a result, David confronted the giant and won.

We, too, will defeat our giants and win if we do what David did. David's faith was not in himself or those around him but in God. Faith in God is an audacious, defiant faith. *"What shall we then say to these things? If God be for us, who can be against us?"* Romans 8:31 (KJV)

David's confidence was rooted squarely in God. He had a deep, abiding relationship with God, one that developed through experience and seeing God work in his life and deliver him from great difficulties. But what do you do when you are just getting to know God, or you don't know him at all? What do you do when you have failed God, yet you come to the place where you desperately need Him and will not find relief at all without divine intervention from God? The formula is the same: you must have faith in God.

Always remember that God's compassion for us is new every morning. That means that God's mercies towards us are continually refreshed, and it does not run out. That also means that the freshness of God's mercy replaces what could have been His judgment. If you are young in the Lord, know that God is able to do anything that you can ask or even think. Remember also that God qualifies us; we do not qualify ourselves. When God declares us worthy, we are worthy. We are because He declared it so.

"Now unto him, that is able to do exceeding abundantly above all that we ask or think, according to the power that worketh in us" (Ephesians 3:20, KJV).

It is of the LORD'S mercies that we are not consumed,
because his compassions fail not.
They are new every morning: great is thy faithfulness.
The LORD is my portion, saith my soul; therefore will I hope in him.

The LORD is good unto them that wait for him, to the soul that seeketh him.
It is good that a man should both hope and quietly wait for the salvation of the LORD.
Lamentations 3:22–26 (KJV)

So no matter who you are or what you have done, you go to God. God always honors the faith we place in Him. The key to it all is faith in God; that is our hope; it is our confidence, and it is our blessed assurance.

Let me illustrate this by looking at an event that is recorded in Matthew 15:22–28. There was a woman that Jesus ignored and whose existence he refused to even acknowledge. This woman's response to Jesus is a case study in the use of aggressive faith. The kind of belief in God that will enable us to press through opposition, rejection, hopelessness, despair, and anything that seeks to get us to give up and turn away from God and the things we need or want.

First, why would Jesus ignore and show such seeming tactlessness? Why would Jesus express such a total lack of regard for someone that came to Him for help? We have to go back a long way and into much history for the complete story. This woman should not even be in existence, let alone have a child. She was a Gentile, and Jews had enormous disdain for Gentiles. She was also a descendent of a people that was so vile that while preparing Israel to enter the promised land, God commanded Israel to kill all of them: every man, woman, and child. They worshiped idols, performed ritual prostitution, and even offered their children as human sacrifices. Small wonder why Jesus used the metaphor of dogs when responding to her.

Their survival was only due to Israel's disobedience. Now, this lady had the audacity to come to the one that spoke forth her destruction to ask for deliverance for her daughter. Now that's bold, risk-taking aggressiveness. That's aggressiveness put forth to receive something being "hoped for." With that bit of history in mind, I'm including the text of this scripture found in Matthew 15:22–28 (KJV).

Aggressiveness is putting forth the confidence, determination, energy, and forcefulness necessary for us to believe God to receive, accomplish, or possess the thing or things being "hoped for."

If this woman didn't have the necessary confidence, she would not have come to Jesus in the first place. Her confidence, however, wasn't self-centered confidence that she was going to get Jesus to do what she wanted; her confidence was that Jesus could do what she wanted.

This woman had faith in God, not that God would but that God could. Once she resolved that portion, the determination, energy, and forcefulness were directed towards getting Jesus to do what she wanted or to get Him, not just to reject her but to deny her. Look closely at the scriptures; the disciples rejected her; Jesus rejected her as well and did so several times. Never, however, did Jesus nor His disciples deny her. That lack of denial left the door open for her to get what she sought.

This little nuance is a subtle example of why intelligence is key to faith. This woman pressed Jesus, not through confidence in her ability to talk Jesus into doing what she wanted but in her confidence that Jesus could do it. That is undeniable, unmitigated faith in God! When Jesus saw that faith, He could say but one thing, "*...woman, great is thy faith: be it unto thee even as thou wilt.*"

True faith is always appropriately and sufficiently aggressive.

When necessary, it will manifest and deploy the appropriate aggressiveness needed to power through the inevitable challenges that stand between God, you, and the things being "hoped for."

Action Plan 3: The Lord Does the Work

"And Joshua said unto them, Fear not, nor be dismayed, be strong and of good courage: for thus shall the LORD do to all your enemies against whom ye fight." Joshua 10:25 (KJV)

"But thanks be to God, which giveth us the victory through our Lord Jesus Christ." First Corinthians 15:57 (KJV)

When acting in accordance with God's will and directions, we show up for the battle in the natural, but the Lord is at work in the realm of the spirit. Things move from spirit to natural. When we act in oneness with God, even when seeking the things we are hoping for or fighting against that by which we are being challenged, it is God that does the work. Our feet may be moving, our arms may be swinging, our tongues wagging, but the Lord is working in the realm of the spirit while we work in the natural, resulting in victory.

Read chapter 10 of Joshua to see how God fought great battles for Israel. You should also see Joshua and Israel doing their part. In fact, other than the hailstones, to the natural eye, it would look like Israel was doing all the work.

In the battle, the role of God is a spiritual role that must manifest itself in the natural. The key for the believer is to do what they do in the natural in sync and in agreement with what the Lord is doing in the spirit realm. The Scripture describes Him as "the

Lord of Hosts," meaning Lord of armies. In our battles, we operate as a division of God's army. We must operate in sync with Him; we must follow His commands, not our own.

This is a part of what Jesus was saying in *"Verily I say unto you, Whatsoever ye shall bind on earth shall be bound in heaven: and whatsoever ye shall loose on earth shall be loosed in heaven."* Matthew 18:18 (KJV)

During the conflict, the Lord empowers and equips us, a division of His army. As we go into battle, He goes ahead of us to prepare, seek, and destroy. None of what God does, however, is codified until we move in agreement with what God is doing. Everything is established through agreement. When the things we say and do are in agreement with what the Lord is doing in the spirit, victory is always assured.

So when you face your challenges, always operate in total agreement with God. Doing so secures your victory, no matter who or what has come against you. The real work is done off-camera, in the spiritual realm, not in the natural realm; it is manifested, however, in the natural.

Do the following when facing your challenge:

- realize and operate as the natural division of God's army;
- seek God's guidance;
- do what God directs you to do;
- allow your actions to be governed by God, not by your natural senses;
- do whatever you do in F.A.I.T.H.;

- timely execute God's directives;
- operate in total agreement with God;
- don't stop until you see in the natural total victory;
- never give up.

You may need to redirect or adjust your efforts, but never ever give up. You do not lose until you do. So don't. It may and even likely will get a lot tougher, but *don't give up!*

Know that when you operate in agreement with God, your hands are God's hands; your ways and all that you do are God's. Stay in agreement with him and be aggressive in doing so.

When walking in faith with God, you will need to be, and in fact must be, confrontationally tenacious, energetic, and engaging. You must bring to bear, through divine guidance, the determination, energy, and forcefulness necessary to receive, accomplish, and possess the thing or things "hoped for" while ensuring that you establish, keep, and maintain your place and position in God. To do so, you will need the aggressiveness of faith.

True faith is always appropriately and sufficiently aggressive. When necessary, it will manifest and deploy the appropriate aggressiveness needed to power through the inevitable challenges that will seek to stand between God, the believer, and the things being "hoped for."

When being aggressive in faith, be confident, not in your ability only but in your ability through God to act, react, and do. Be confident to do your part in achieving the victories you need through God.

When being aggressive in faith, be determined, willing to challenge confidently, energetically, and forcefully that which challenges you, your confidence in God, and that which challenges God's will for your life.

The aggressiveness of faith is used to:

1. establish the will of God;
2. allow God to act through us to establish His will;
3. make us willing, through God, to challenge that which challenges us;
4. motivate us to put forth the efforts that are necessary to establish the will, plan, and purpose of God.

Faith Is Always Intelligent

...it is given unto you to
know the mysteries of the kingdom
of heaven, but to them it is not given.
But blessed are your eyes, for
they see: and your ears, for they hear.
But he that received seed into
the good ground is he that heareth
the word, and understandeth it...
Matthew 13:11, 16, 23 (KJV)

CHAPTER 7:

THE INTELLIGENCE OF FAITH

Intelligence. True faith is always intelligent. The intelligence of faith is making the connection between what God has done for you previously and what you are believing Him to do presently. It is resolving in your heart and mind that if He did it once, He can and will do it again in your present situation.

Secondly, the intelligence of faith is seeing the mind of God in each situation or circumstance while operating in agreement with God, not the situation or circumstance.

Thirdly, the intelligence of faith is seeing God at work in your life or in the lives of others, then using that awareness and the knowledge to believe God for something else, even something greater than before.

Seemingly, too many believers believe that thinking equates to doubt and should never enter into the process of exercising faith. That is the farthest thing from the truth. In fact, I say, when it comes to the things you are hoping for, not correlating relevant past experiences will produce ignorance, a lack of awareness that will not yield faith but instead fear, doubt, and foolishness.

It is essential that we see what God has done and is doing.

Doing so enables us to believe Him for what He is yet to do. That's what David did when confronting the Philistine champion and giant, Goliath. David was convinced that although he was a young shepherd boy, he could defeat that seasoned man of war. Many saw Goliath not only being larger than life but also invincible. But to David, it was just a matter of time before his head would be in his hands and vultures were feeding upon his corpse.

Unlike others, David reasoned, "*The LORD that delivered me out of the paw of the lion, and out of the paw of the bear, will deliver me out of the hand of this Philistine.*"

It is critically important that believers objectively see God at work in their lives and use what He has done and is doing to develop a relationship with God that will create the certainty that He will do for them the things that seem to be impossible. That's what David did, and that's what we must do. That process was the basis for David's soundness and confidence. That confidence was rooted squarely in his F.A.I.T.H. in God.

> *"David said moreover, The LORD that delivered me out of the paw of the lion, and out of the paw of the bear, he will deliver me out of the hand of this Philistine. And Saul said unto David, Go, and the LORD be with thee."*
> *First Samuel 17:37 (KJV)*

Using Intelligence to See God

Through those few verses, we see that David realized that it was not his ability but God's ability that gave him the victory over both the lion and bear. As a result, David concluded that God would do the same when he confronted Goliath.

David's faith was not rooted in his abilities. He knew that by far, he wasn't physically as strong as the lion or bear. David saw God at work in those situations and attributed his success to God. As a result, he concluded that God would do the same with Goliath. That is the intelligence of faith in operation.

Has God delivered you from something that was greater than you? Has He brought you through that which seemed to be impossible? I am sure He has, but did you conclude that it was God that delivered you, or did you decide that it was your skill, education, luck, fate, etc., that brought you through? If in your heart, mind, and soul, you did not conclude that it was God that delivered you, you missed an opportunity to grow in your faith intelligence. Faith intelligence must be developed. It is developed through developing a personal relationship with God and giving Him credit for what He does.

The intelligence of faith will always bring you into a place of faith in God. Such faith will become easy as you begin to see and acknowledge the things that the Lord does in your life.

Natural intelligence is the collection of information and the application of knowledge and skills. The intelligence that brings us to faith does the same thing; we gather the information that serves as evidence that it could only have been God that was working in and through your life while facing your challenges.

> *"Now faith is the substance of things hoped for, the evidence of things not seen." Hebrews 11:1 (KJV)*

Gathering the information that leads us to the conclusion that it could only have been God at work, not us, becomes our evidence that God will do the same during our present situation. That resulting confidence in God will then become the substance *(basis)* for our hope that God will do it in our current situation. Faith is not the assurance that what we want will happen; it is confidence in God that He is able regardless of what does or does not happen. That is indeed that intelligence of faith.

The intelligence of faith brings us to the conclusion that our deliverance was not due to our gifting or all of the other things that we may have done but was instead due to what God has done. It is foolish to conclude otherwise.

Intelligence works with faith, not against it, and should be seen in that context. The intelligence of faith helps to bolster our faith in God, not diminish it. Intelligence is the aspect of faith that allows us to recognize what God has done or is doing. It also establishes the basis for our trust in God to do, in the present, what we are hoping for. The intelligence of faith can also help us determine if we are losing focus by referencing what God has done previously, helping us to acquire and maintain bearing.

Using Intelligence to Get to Faith

In Matthew 8:5–13, a Roman centurion had a servant that was very ill. He came *(or sent)* to Jesus, asking Him to heal his servant. Jesus agreed, expressing that He would come to his home to do so. The centurion, insisting that he was not worthy of Jesus coming to his home, asked Jesus to give the order, and his servant would be healed.

The centurion, *using intelligence gained from his own experiences as an officer*, deduced that if Jesus simply gave the order, his servant would be healed.

That event is an example of how a man without a personal relationship with God could look at how Jesus exercised His authority, then use that information to conclude that Jesus could heal his servant by giving the order. The centurion used carnal knowledge and logic to bring him to the place of great faith. That approach was natural, militaristic, and drawn from past experiences, but it brought him to a place of great faith, a greatness of faith not seen at the time among God's people. The centurion's faith brought him to a place where he believed that if he could get Jesus to give the order, then his servant would be healed.

The centurion's approach illustrates that there is a principle to faith that will work for anyone, regardless of their relationship to or position with God. One does not have to be saved, free from sin, or in a particular group to walk in faith. It is not to say that those things are not important on some level, but not as it relates to faith. Faith will work in any life and in any situation.

Let me pause just a bit to say that this centurion's logic, other than getting Jesus to speak the word only, was not used to determine how the healing process should unfold, be carried out, nor for that matter, when and how things could or should not be done. The centurion reasoned that Jesus could do what he needed to be done. He also concluded that Jesus could do it anytime He chose. That was true faith in God.

As believers, we must learn to trust the Lord with the details. The whens, hows, wherefores, etc., should be left to God. He knows how to bring about our deliverance. This doesn't mean that we do not ask or express our desires and desperations fervently. As the psalmist wrote, "*Make haste, O God, to deliver me; make haste to help me, O LORD*" (Psalm 70:1, 5, 40:13, KJV).

The centurion reasoned, after seeing and hearing about Jesus, that Jesus could simply speak the word, and his servant would be healed. The centurion's understanding of authority concluded that Jesus had the authority; he was not trying to control how things should be done. He was saying, in essence, "I believe You have the authority, so if You give the order, my servant will be healed." The centurion's reasoning was militaristic, simple, no-nonsense, and straightforward. You have the authority, give the order, and my servant will be healed. Done! That is faith in God fueled by intelligence.

If I may add, anyone can use the centurion's approach to get faith in God. What was that approach? Look at what God has done, look at what God is doing, then conclude that God can and will do the same in your situation; that is the intelligence of faith.

When Jesus heard the centurion's rationale, He was amazed. He was amazed because the centurion was able to do something that His disciples and all of those in Israel hadn't done in all of the time He spent with them. The centurion was able to put things together and correlate one miracle to the next and deduce that something else could be done. That is the intelligence of faith, and that was the place where Jesus was desperately trying to get His disciples: to see one thing, then believe that the next is possible. Jesus was trying to get His disciples to use logic to get faith in God. The story began in Matthew 14:14–21 and continued in 15:32–38, but consider what Jesus told them in Matthew 16:5–12; I've included verses 7–11 (KJV):

> *And they reasoned among themselves, saying, It is because we have taken no bread. Which when Jesus perceived, he said unto them, O ye of little faith, why reason ye among yourselves, because ye have brought no bread? Do ye not yet understand, neither remember the five loaves of the five thousand, and how many baskets ye took up? Neither the seven loaves of the four thousand, and how many baskets ye took up? How is it that ye do not understand that I spake it not to you*

concerning bread, that ye should beware of the leaven of the Pharisees and of the Sadducees?

We see through those scriptures that Jesus wanted His disciples to understand what He did, and He expected them to learn to do them. Jesus wanted the disciples to do what the centurion did and more. The centurion was a man that had no relationship with God and admittedly lived life in such a way that he felt unworthy to even allow Jesus into his house. Should not the people of God, those that have a relationship with God, be able to do the same and more? Jesus wanted His disciples to logically look at what He was doing and then do it themselves. He wants us to do the same.

The lesson of the disciples is our lesson. Don't limit yourself to your natural abilities or to what you see in the natural. Believe God for more and do more.

Jesus directed His disciples to do one thing before He fed the thousands. He told the disciples, "Give you them to eat." Jesus was telling them to tap into their supernatural abilities to feed thousands. He did so in Matthew 14:16, Mark 6:37, and Luke 9:13. In each instance, Jesus told His disciples, "Give you them to eat." If you see the need, exercise faith in God yourself. You give them something to eat.

Jesus was telling the disciples to believe and trust God to feed the thousands through and by their own hands. He, in essence, was saying, "Don't just depend on the Father to use Me. Allow Him to use you." Respond in faith and not by what you see in the natural. Remember what God has done and believe Him for more. Have faith in God.

True faith in God is not blind; it is not ignorant, and it sure isn't foolish. True faith in God doesn't ignore intellect, nor does it allow intellect to dictate outcomes solely. Faith in God harnesses intelligence to do things that cannot be done otherwise.

Faith in God is always intelligent, but the intelligence of faith cannot always be seen or comprehended by the natural mind. The natural mind calls the incomprehensible a miracle; the spiritual mind calls it a manifestation of faith. Never forget that true faith is always intelligent.

One more thing: The disciples (*while with Jesus*) were unsaved; the centurion and everyone that Jesus told to believe or that He healed, etc., were all unsaved. None of them were filled with the Holy Spirit. None of them had then what believers have now. Believers today have salvation and the Holy Spirit indwelling them. Jesus seemed to have suggested that we could see God do greater works in and through our lives if we simply believed Him to do so. If we accept and expect that He can and will, He will.

We today view the miracles that Jesus performed as being possible only due to Jesus being the Son of God. To which I say, "Hogwash." Who are we? What does the Scripture say about us? "*Beloved, now are we the sons of God, and it doth not yet appear what we shall be: but we know that, when he shall appear, we shall be like him; for we shall see him as he is*" (1 John 3:2, KJV). We, too, are sons of God if we have accepted Jesus as Lord and Savior of our lives. We can and should do more.

As it relates to miracles being done through God's people, we see recorded during Old Testament periods miracles similar to what Jesus did in the New Testament. The replenishing oil and meal at the word of Elijah in 1 Kings chapter 17. Elijah raising the widow's son from the dead also in 1 Kings chapter 17 and many, many more.

We do ourselves a disservice by chalking up the miracles of

Jesus to Him being the Son of God. Doing so insulates us from Jesus and the examples that He was setting for us to follow. Jesus said that we would do what He did and more, "*Verily, verily, I say unto you, He that believeth on me, the works that I do shall he do also; and greater works than these shall he do; because I go unto my Father*" (John 14:12, KJV).

Jesus said it perfectly in John 14:12. There, Jesus lets us know two things: (1) if we believe Him, we can do what He did; (2) as a result of Him going back to the Father, we would do greater things than He was doing at the time.

Before the crucifixion, men walked with God, and the Spirit of God worked among them. After the crucifixion and resurrection, believers can have the Spirit of God dwell within them. As believers, we can be at one with God, and we can be at one in God through His Spirit. We can have the Spirit of God not only dwell within us but also work through us, doing His will. Whether New Testament or Old, the times of Jesus or our times, it is the Holy Spirit that does the work. It is the Holy Spirit that heals the sick, raises the dead, etc.

When looking at the things that Jesus did while on earth, believers should consider those things to be the least that they can do. Once any of us receives the Spirit of God and begins to walk in the Spirit, the "greater works than these" principle applies to our lives. Remember, however, that it is the Spirit of God that does the work through us, in accord with God's will, not ours. It is God's grace and our faith in God that initiate the process.

The intelligence of faith is seeing the works of God, then coming to know the mind of God in each situation and circumstance while operating in agreement with God. The intelligence of faith is also exercising the ability to acquire and apply the knowledge and skills necessary through the Spirit of God to accomplish and possess the things "hoped for."

True faith is always intelligent, helping us to see the Lord at work in our lives, enabling us to believe God for even greater things. The intelligence of faith always results in an ever-increasing faith in God. The intelligence of faith will truly make F.A.I.T.H. in God much, much easier.

Action Plan 4: Take Note of What God Has Done

By faith Abraham, when he was tried, offered up Isaac: and he that had received the promises offered up his only begotten son, Of whom it was said, That in Isaac shall thy seed be called: Accounting that God was able to raise him up, even from the dead; from whence also he received him in a figure. Hebrews 11:17–19 (KJV):

When believing God, don't abandon your intellect, but never allow intellect to interfere with what God is doing or wants to do in your life or in the earth. Learn to use intelligence and allow it to help you see and understand what God has done in your life and in the lives of others. Allow the knowledge and understanding gained from past experiences to help you solidify your faith in God. Abraham did that, enabling him to become a great man of faith.

Abraham's faith was illustrated when God told him to offer up his son Isaac as a sacrifice to God. Abraham had no second thoughts as to whether or not he would do so. He did not have any concerns because of his past experiences with God and because of what God promised him.

Because of his relationship with God, Abraham knew that God would do what He promised. God said that Isaac was the seed of promise. Abraham, having that knowledge, concluded that if he killed Isaac, God would have to raise him from the dead in order to keep His promise. Today we know the rest of the story, but at that time, Abraham depended upon the intelligence of faith.

To strengthen your faith, you must bring to memory the things that God has done in your life and what He has done in the lives of others. God has no respect of persons. Reflecting and meditating upon what God has done can help you to believe God for bigger and greater things. That, too, is the intelligence of faith.

"Meditate upon these "things; give thyself wholly to them; "that thy profiting may appear to all."
First Timothy 4:15 (KJV):

A Final Thought

It's important to note that the intelligence of faith will not only help you see the Lord at work in your life; it will also show you what your adversary, the devil, may have done or might be doing in your life and in the earth.

Allow the Spirit of God to reveal to you who and what may be working for or against you in this life; doing so will help you to walk in total victory in every area of your life. That is truly the intelligence of faith.

Faith Is Always Tenacious

"Let us hold fast the profession
"of our faith without wavering;
"(for he is faithful that promised)."
Hebrews 10:23 (KJV)

CHAPTER 8:

THE TENACIOUSNESS OF FAITH

Tenacious. True faith is always tenacious. The tenaciousness of faith is not giving in, not giving up, not giving out, and not going away. It's being relentless and doggedly determined to hang in there until you do whatever is necessary to achieve what you're hoping for. The key to the tenaciousness of faith is consistently moving in the direction necessary to accomplish the objective.

One day while traveling in my trusty 1990 Chevy pickup, I saw a sign that read, "Roadwork Ahead, Detour." I then saw an arrow pointing in the direction I must turn. I followed the direction of the detour. Even though the route I then was traveling was not as direct as intended, I was yet moving toward my destination. Originally, I was headed south; the detour directed me west. No matter the direction, west, east, north, south, I was headed to my destination.

What I was doing seemed counter to reaching my objective, but there was one constant: my mind. My original intentions did not change. My mind, focus, intentions, desires were all intact; they never changed. No matter the turn, I was still heading toward my objective.

The obstacles forced me to adjust, but they did not deter me from reaching my objective. I was tenacious. The more turns I made, the more relentless, determined, and persistent I became. Nothing deterred me from reaching my destination. That's what we do when walking in faith. No matter the challenge, no matter the hindrances, we do not abandon the things for which we hope.

Faith doesn't allow obstacles, impediments, or anything else to change our confidence in God. Every action, every change of direction, thought, or idea is tied to reaching the objective. Always move forward. Hold fast and remain committed to doing whatever it takes in God to reach the objective.

In Luke 5:18–26, a group of men carried another man on a stretcher to be healed by Jesus. The man was suffering from a sickness called palsy. Arriving at the place where Jesus was, there were so many people there that they could not get anywhere near Jesus.

The men then changed strategy, but not their objective. They maneuvered to the building where Jesus was and climbed onto the roof. Once on the rooftop, they determined Jesus' location within the building, removed the roofing tiles, and lowered the man to Jesus from the roof to be healed.

I can only imagine what may have gone through Jesus' mind while teaching the multitude or healing the sick when suddenly debris from the roof began falling upon him. Imagine Jesus looking up when all of a sudden light began to shine through the tiles, and a person on a stretcher began to be lowered, landing in front of Him. Imagine Jesus laying hands upon the man, healing him, and then looking up at the men on the roof, saying, "Guys, it was your faith that got this man his healing."

In fact, if there ever was an example of someone's tenaciousness, what they did on that man's behalf was it. Those men gathered this sick man from wherever he was at the time to bring him to Jesus. The scripture doesn't tell us how far they traveled or whether or not they were around the corner. Whatever the case, these men got to that place and found that there were so many people there that there were little hopes of getting anywhere near Jesus through that crowd. They didn't give up or take a chance on waiting. If Jesus left, their efforts would be in vain.

Somehow they got the bright idea of doing what no one else had done. They developed a roof entry strategy and executed it. How innovative. Sometimes to accomplish great things, we must do what has never been done before. That requires tenacious faith.

Imagine the obstacles those men may have gone through to get that man on to and through the roof and then to Jesus. The tenaciousness of faith considers the obstacles but doesn't allow them to stop forward progress. Tenaciousness is always forward-moving. Tenacious faith looks beyond the obstacles to target a path that will enable the obstacles to be overcome and the objective to be reached. That's what we should do while having faith in God.

True faith is always tenacious; it is relentlessly determined to receive the thing being hoped for. The key to tenacious faith is to move consistently, relentlessly, and continually along the path that leads to the place where you will accomplish your objective. There is an answer to every problem or dilemma. Tenacious faith provides the fuel you will need to discover it. Everything you do, however, must be done in accordance with the will, plan, and purpose of God.

In Luke 18:1–8, Jesus told the story of a woman that confronted victimization, injustice, self-righteousness, and condescension. He indicated that her persistence is what enabled her to receive the relief she sought.

When we read this parable, we focus primarily on the woman's persistence in returning over and over again to an unjust judge in an effort to get him to grant her petition. In reality, this parable wasn't as much about wearing out the judge as it was her continuing to bring her request before him. Let's look at the verses. Luke 18:1–8 (KJV):

> *And he spake a parable unto them to this end, that men ought always to pray, and not to faint;*
>
> *Saying, There was in a city a judge, which feared not God, neither regarded man:*
>
> *And there was a widow in that city; and she came unto him, saying, Avenge me of mine adversary. And he would not for a while: but afterward he said within himself, Though I fear not God, nor regard man;*
>
> *Yet because this widow troubleth me, I will avenge her, lest by her continual coming she weary me. And the Lord said, Hear what the unjust judge saith. And shall not God avenge his own elect, which cry day and night unto him, though he bear long with them?*
>
> *I tell you that he will avenge them speedily. Nevertheless when the Son of man cometh, shall he find faith on the earth?*

The premise of the above parable is stated in verse one. In the verse, Jesus outlined two things: First, the importance of continual prayer. He said that "*…men ought always to pray…*" Secondly, the importance of being tenacious. Don't ever give up. Jesus said that men should always pray and also not faint (*lose heart, give up, etc.*). In other words, pray tenaciously.

Prayer should always be accompanied by tenacious faith. Remember the prayer of faith is always tenacious. This is the message that Jesus was trying to get across to those of His day, and it is the message He is trying to get across to us. We must be tenacious in prayer. We should never give up.

Consider this: Why are you trying to have faith in the first place? To get what you are hoping for. Right? Now, why do you want whatever you are hoping for? Is it because you don't have it? Of course. So why do you not have it? Because you do not have the means, ability, or knowledge to acquire it or to resolve the issues and circumstances surrounding its acquisition.

If something in that little scenario weren't the case, you would, in all likelihood, have what you are hoping for and not be seeking it. That's why tenaciousness is essential to both faith and prayer. James 4:2 (KJV) says, *"...[you] have not because ye ask not."* Proverbs 3:6 (KJV) says, *"In all [our] ways, acknowledge Him and He shall direct [your] path."* The process of acquiring the things we hope for should always begin by asking, not asking anyone but asking God. Often, we step out without recognizing that God must play a role in our receiving the things for which we hope.

When we start the process without asking the Lord or acknowledging Him, we are saying by default, "I can do this one without Him." Or "I am going to do this my way." Either way, you have the right to do so, but doing so increases your possibility of failure, no matter how hard you work at it.

Tenaciousness without prayer is just hard work. It's a laborious, intensive, carnal effort. The results may be your best, but it may not be God's best for you if He isn't involved in the process.

When we seek and obey God's directions, we move into

partnership and agreement with Him. When that happens, we can't fail. But never do so out of formality or routine. That would not be a true agreement. Do so with conscious awareness and commitment to act in perfect accord and approval of your principal partner, God.

The second thing Jesus was saying while telling the story of the woman is that praying should be tenacious. In Christian circles, there is a tendency to believe that if they ask more than once, their continual asking is an indication of a lack of faith or even doubt. It could be, but not necessarily.

Jesus seems to be saying that there is merit to continually asking and that doing so can be an indication of faith, not a lack of it.

In the parable, Jesus seems to be saying, pray until you get what you are hoping for, not just until you are certain that you are heard. Doing that is truly tenacious faith. There is little wrong with praying to God until you receive the manifestation. Doing so is saying, "God, I know You can do what I am asking." Why won't or shouldn't you?

I know that some believe that one should never question God, but that simply is not biblically accurate. Why would God instruct us to ask but not allow us to question? Why would He say in James 1:5 (KJV) that "*If any man lacks wisdom, let him ask God…*"? In addition, there are countless examples in Scripture to the contrary. We even saw Jesus, who was perfect in His relationship with the Father, question the Father. Jesus Christ is our perfect example in all things.

Allow me to be a little redundant. The mere fact that you, I, or anyone else keep asking God or keep coming back to Him, as in the case of the woman with the judge, is an indication of faith, not a lack of it. The continual coming back indicates confidence that you believe the one you are asking can do what you ask. Think about it this way: Why keep coming back if you know you will never get the person to grant your request?

If you wanted to ask a person for something and were certain the person would not grant your request, would you ask the person anyway? Some would, but I guess that most would not. If you asked the person and they said no or ignored you as if you had never asked, would you continue to ask? I say most would not. Some may come initially, and some may even come back twice, but it is unlikely that they would continue to come after such denials. That is, if they are convinced that the request will never be granted.

Jesus instructs, *"...that men ought always to pray, and not to faint"* (Luke 18:1, KJV). The word "ought" in the original text indicates a necessary behavior or need. Jesus is saying this is the pattern, position, and approach that we should take in prayer. He is saying, "Be tenacious, don't lose heart, don't give up." Jesus is letting us know that coming back is not an indication of a lack of faith but rather an indication *of* our faith.

So keep asking until you see God work in your situation. Keep coming back because you know that God can and will do what you are asking. If nothing else, your continual coming to God is an indication that you haven't given up on God.

One last thing as it relates to asking in faith. It is said that if you asked once and believe that you have it, there is no need for you to ask again. That could be true, but sometimes the confidence of knowing your request has been or will be granted will produce an enthusiasm that will produce an eager, continual asking of when.

It's like promising a child something that they want badly. They will bug you until they receive the complete manifestation of what was promised. There isn't a thing wrong with a believer doing the same thing. If, like the child, that believer is asking as a result of faith. The difference in asking in faith and not is that one is asking if, while the other is asking when.

In Revelation 6:9–11, the souls under the altar of God continually asked how long. In the case of the woman and the unjust judge and the souls under the altar of God, the continual asking was not due to doubt but rather confidence that the one being asked did hear and would answer.

> *And this is the confidence that we have in him, that, if we ask any thing according to his will, he heareth us: And if we know that he hear us, whatsoever we ask, we know that we have the petitions that we desired of him.*
> *First John 5:14–15 (KJV)*

So if you ask God multiple times, let it be a tenacious faith asking. The kind of asking where the one asking knows that the one being asked can, and will, give that for which is being asked.

There are two other things that Jesus seems to be saying in this parable: First, our heavenly Father is not an unjust judge. He will not put us through unnecessary waiting and begging. It is His good pleasure to give us what we ask, and He will do so as quickly as practical. That's the confident trust that every believer should have in their heavenly Father.

It is also important to note that there is a difference between tenaciousness and begging. Tenaciousness will always be rooted in confident determination, while begging is rooted in hopelessness and despair. Believers are never without hope. As the psalmist expressed, we "hope in God." In Psalm 37:25 (KJV), David wrote, *"I have been young, and now am old; yet have I not seen the righteous forsaken, nor his seed begging bread."* God also gave us this promise, *"And this is the confidence that we have in him, that, if we ask any thing according to his will, he heareth us"* (1 John 5:14, KJV).

There is one last thing Jesus wants us to know through the parable in *Luke 18:1–8*: Those whom He has chosen pray to Him continually, and He hears every prayer. He also said that He would answer and do so speedily. God does not always inform us as to why some of our prayers take so long for us to receive the manifestation, but He will always answer. We do know, however, that His ways and His thoughts are exceedingly higher than ours. This is why we must trust Him, trust in Him, and trust in His will.

Continue to trust, continue to believe, continue to be tenacious. Faith in God is always tenacious.

Action Plan 5: Don't Give Up, Get There

Brethren, I count not myself to have apprehended: but this one thing I do, forgetting those things which are behind, and reaching forth unto those things which are before, I press toward the mark for the prize of the high calling of God in Christ Jesus.
Philippians 3:13–14 (KJV)

Action 5a. Never Give Up, Never Give In, Never Give Out

There is a bit of advice and direction that I want to give everyone called by the name of our Lord: Never give up, never give in, never give out. If what you are hoping for is worth desiring, it's worth the fight. It's also worth the persistence needed to bring it about. Enter the press, always press forward. Again, never give up. Never give in. Never give out.

Be tenacious. Endure the challenges that stand between you and your victory. Press through life's difficulties with confidence and zeal. Know that the Lord will always keep His promises.

Action 5b. Move beyond Endurance

Please understand that tenaciousness is not an endurance contest. You will never outlast the devil, but you can and will defeat him if you do not give up. Endurance is important, but it will rarely yield the victory needed to overcome a formable adversary like the devil. If the devil is holding up a victory or blessing, he will not feel sorry for you and release it. When confronting the devil, you must be consistently, relentlessly engaged in an effort to defeat him. You must also activate and deploy a tenacious, determined, focused faith.

Action 5c. Be an Overcomer

Endurance is usually a defensive measure that should only be viewed as a temporary exercise, even if used offensively. You must overcome the devil's challenges. He attempts to rob, steal, kill, and destroy you or that for which you are hoping. If you don't move into the victory that Christ has accomplished on your behalf, the devil will try to destroy you. Don't let him.

Through sufficient application of God's Word and yielding to the Holy Spirit, you can move into the victories that Christ has won for you. Never try to confront the devil through your strength and means alone. Seek God first, place your resources under His command, then yield to His guidance. That is what His Word says to do. If you do that, you will overcome every challenge of the devil and inhabit the victory that Christ has given you.

Action 5d. Be Willing to Risk It All

Tenaciousness is believing God to the point where you are willing to put everything on the line. You must be willing to risk it all for the Lord, even that which He has given you, even your very life. But do nothing on a whim. Only be led by the Lord. To reach that level of faith, you must believe God. You must learn to hear His voice. If you don't learn His voice, you can easily be deceived by the devil, yourself, or others.

Action 5e. Know that God Cannot and Will Not Lie.

Once you come to know God's Word and His voice, tenacious faith will become easy. It will become easy because, through His Word, you will learn that God cannot and will not lie. Wow! Think about that: God cannot lie. It is truly impossible for Him to do so. As believers, we must exercise the resolve that reflects that truth, and if God says it, God will do it. If God speaks it, God will bring it to pass. We must hold on to that fact tenaciously.

Conclusion

Simply trying to outlast the devil is a flawed strategy, one that usually fails without the intervening grace of God. Your strategy must be based on God's Word and focused not on the circumstances but on what God said.

Your strategy must be aggressive, deploying the energy necessary to power through every obstacle and challenge necessary to get to the things you hope for. Don't be arrogant, be resolute and committed to doing what's necessary to receive what God has promised.

Your strategy must be intelligent, not fantasy. You must realize that God can indeed do anything, but should He? This intelligence is not based on or derived from carnal headiness. It is from the mind of God. It may even seem foolish by some standards, but it is an intelligence that a carnal, fleshly intellect cannot receive or comprehend.

The tenaciousness of faith's strategy must also be humble to keep the one using it open and sensitive to the Spirit of God. Those walking in faith must see God and yield to His insights, guidance, and directions. They must do so tenaciously.

The tenaciousness of faith is being relentless and doggedly determined to hang in there to do whatever is necessary until the thing or things being "hoped for" are achieved. True faith has always been and will always be tenacious.

Faith Is Always Humble

For whosoever exalteth
himself shall be abased;
and he that humbleth
himself shall be exalted.
Luke 14:11 (KJV)

CHAPTER 9:

THE HUMILITY OF FAITH

Humble. The key to faith is having faith in God. The key to faith in God is believing God to the point where you are committed to accepting and establishing God's will over your own will. To do that, you must have absolute trust in God. It's easy to submit to God's will if you have total trust in God.

One of the greatest impediments to our faith in God is a lack of trust in God. Building trust in God requires the development of a relationship with God. Developing such a relationship requires humble obedience to God. It's only then that one can believe God to the point where they are willing to place God's will above their own. Doing so is truly the "humility of faith."

The "humility of faith" is humble obedience to God. Living a life of humility does two things: First, it prevents us from becoming arrogant and pretentious. Secondly, it makes it possible for us to surrender our will to God's will, resulting in a higher, more consistent level of obedience to God.

If a person is not living life in obedience to God or is arrogant or exercises faith to impress, that person is operating in carnality. Such a person does not have faith in God. They may have confidence, but is that confidence self-confidence or confidence in God?

I am not saying that self-confidence is bad. I am saying that, ideally, self-confidence should always be rooted in being God confident. If not, when situations overwhelm your self-confidence, you will have nothing to sustain yourself.

Misplaced self-confidence will usually produce arrogance and self-exhortation. Such will eventually hinder, if not undermine, a person's walk with God. That's why humility and faith in God are so important.

True faith in God is always humble. It can be questioned as to whether or not faith void of humility is true faith in God. It may indeed be what we consider to be faith, but is it true faith in God? I submit to you that it is unlikely that it is.

If God exalts the humble and brings low the self-exalted, how then can faith that is void of humility truly be faith in God?

The humility of faith preserves the confidence of faith while being aware of and considerate of God's divine will, plan, purpose, and how faith's actions may affect others. At the same time, however, faith's humility does not ignore the needs, wants, or desires of the one that possesses it.

It's vitally important that every believer walks in humility. It's a must, and it is impossible to have and walk in true faith in God without the humility of faith.

The Meekness of Humility

During His sermon on the mount, Jesus declared that there were several conditions of man's heart that would yield the divine favor (blessings) of God. One of them was meekness. He said in Matthew 5:5 (KJV), "*Blessed are the meek: for they shall inherit the earth.*" In the original Greek text, the word "meek" in this verse could also have been translated as "the humble."

Jesus is saying that those that live in respectful submission and obedience to God have the favor of God upon their lives. They, the humble, will be the ones that inherit the earth. Why? Because of their humble obedience to the will of their heavenly Father and their willingness to submit their own will to God's will. That is indeed faith in God, and that is what is meant by the meekness of humility.

Humility gives faith its temperament and balance. The lack of humility has caused some to wreak havoc when operating in traditional approaches to faith. A lack of humility makes it easy to get caught up in the moment. It may also blind the person to things of which they should be aware.

It was necessary for Jesus to teach His disciples how to operate in faith coupled with humility. We see an example of this when John told Jesus that he forbade a man from casting out devils because the man wasn't one of Jesus' disciples. Jesus instructed him not to do so because if the man wasn't working against Him, he was working with Him. Such is difficult to grasp when looking at things with a carnal bent or based upon one's religious beliefs.

Not long after that, Jesus knew it was about time to offer Himself up. He and His disciples began to walk to Jerusalem. He sent disciples ahead of Him to find a place to spend the night. Those disciples entered a village of the Samaritans, who refused to let them stay after discovering that they were headed to Jerusalem. When James and John found out, they wanted to call fire from heaven to burn them up. Jesus, in the scripture, says, "*…turned, and rebuked them, and said, Ye know not what manner of spirit ye* *are of*" (Luke 9:55, KJV). They then went into another village that accepted them.

The disciples seemed to believe that they had the faith and ability to call fire down from heaven, but they were lacking significantly in faith's humility. Their lack of humility resulted in them being insensitive, even to the need for the villagers to have a future opportunity to be won to Christ or see the will of God manifested in those lives.

Jesus told them in verse 56 (KJV) that "*…the Son of man is not come to destroy men's lives, but to save them.*" Far too often, believers fail to understand that God's desire is for no one to perish but that all men would have eternal life (John 3:15–17). By failing to understand God's heart, often believers do things that are contrary to God's will. Everything that God does on earth is done in hopes of reestablishing a personal and intimate relationship with the ones He loves.

The disciple's lack of humility not only resulted in their insensitivity to the needs of those villagers; it also made them insensitive to the will of God.

Humility is meekness, reflexive obedience to the will of God. It's realized in a responsive temperament, reacting unhesitantly to God's will, not the will of the individual. The humility of faith responds to and yields itself to the desires of our heavenly Father, not our own.

Jesus was our perfect example as to how the humility of faith works. He illustrated it in the garden of Gethsemane. Facing death through crucifixion, Jesus began to pray for the possibility of avoiding that fate. Then realizing that there wasn't, Jesus, being our example, submitted His will, the Father's will.

> *"...fell on his face, and prayed, saying, O my Father, if it be possible, let this cup pass from me: nevertheless not as I will, but as thou wilt" (Matthew 26:39, KJV).*

I'm sure that Jesus had the faith, power, and all else He needed to do whatever He wanted. That meek *(humble)* lamb of God humbled Himself, in oneness, to the Father, allowing Himself to be hung on a cross, not for Himself but for each of us (Philippians 2:8).

Our faith will give us the confidence to get the things we want, but the humility of faith gives us the confidence to give God the things *He* wants. For the believer, that's the choice.

The Humility of Faith (A Product of Love)

The humility of faith is meekness that lies in the hearts of every great man or woman of faith who realizes their need for God. It is rooted in the obedience of love as described by Jesus in Luke 10:27 and John 14:15.

> *"...Thou shalt love the Lord thy God with all thy heart, and with all thy soul, and with all thy strength, and with all thy mind; and thy neighbour as thyself" (Luke 10:27, KJV).*

> *"If ye love me, keep my commandments" (John 14:15, KJV).*

God, not man, sets the standard for man's love for Him. No one can fully know what love is void of a personal, intimate, love relationship with God. Outside of such a relationship, man is incapable of setting a proper standard for love. Man's standard for love is based upon what he sees, feels, hears, knows, or is aware of. God's standard is vastly different. First John 4:8 says that God is love; how then can anyone love outside of God? For man to define love would be for man to define God. God never approved such.

Faith's humility is rooted in a love relationship with God; total obedience to God requires it. For respectful submission and obedience to God to be reflected in our lives, we must have the meekness of humility. Jesus said in John 14:15 that if we love Him, we will do what He commands. Our love for God facilitates our obedience to Him.

When we live lives in obedience to God, doing *His* will and not our own, our obedience to God moves us into a place of agreement with Him. That agreement with God establishes the will of God. It then becomes possible for God's will to be realized and solidified in earth. Our walk of agreement with God ensures constant victory in our lives. It's clear that our walk of agreement with God is key to our faith in God. Faith is truly made easy when we live lives of humility.

One other thing about love, meekness, humility, and obedience as related to faith in God. Those words are commonly mentioned within the context of faith, but if we can come to realize that obedience is key to having faith in God, it will make a lot of sense. Disobedience shows a lack of confidence in the one that should be obeyed. If that's true, how can one have faith in God and act in disobedience to God at the same time? They can't.

So our love for God will manifest itself in our obedience to Him. It doesn't stop there, however. As said earlier, God is love. We can only know, experience, and understand love by first loving God. We then become the first beneficiaries of that love, learning what love is and how to truly love. The process is to first love God, then self, then others. We use our love of self as the basis upon which we judge our love for others. This approach to love removes the self-centeredness that prevents improper considerations that motivate us to take advantage of others. Such expressions of love acknowledge self and the needs of self without allowing the person to become consumed by self.

Without love for God, the person—supposedly walking in faith—may become blinded to the needs of God and others, focusing squarely on their own needs. This approach to faith increases the possibility of being at odds with God and increases the likelihood of frustration when things don't go as planned. Such frustration is usually a result of working against God.

Placing love for God as the foundation for faith in God will bring balance and clarity in one's life, enabling one to be open to God's directions, seeing where He may be leading.

Subordinating self-love to love for God while placing love for others on par with love for self enables us to tenaciously plow through the challenges we face while acquiring the things hoped for and keeping us humble. Properly appropriating our love will also allow the humility of faith to remain at the forefront of our lives and govern our actions.

Humility Realizes the Need for God

The humility of faith also enables us to clearly see the ability and capability of God while at the same time positioning us to enter into oneness with God. Entering oneness with God enables us to tap into resources we do not have. Those resources will provide us the means we need to accomplish the things that we are hoping for. Humility is key to that process. Humility is key to entering into oneness with God.

In Matthew chapter 15, the woman from Canaan displayed the

humility of faith as she sought Jesus on behalf of her daughter. After being told by Jesus that it was not proper to give the children's food to dogs, she responded to Jesus by saying that even dogs are given scraps from their master's table. This woman was confident yet humble enough to not be offended.

We don't realize that often our being offended is a lack of humility. The offense indicates an unsubmitted heart, one that has not embraced an outcome. Being offended can also blind us to alternatives that may enable us to navigate the cause of the offense.

Rather than becoming offended, the woman from Canaan negotiated for leftovers. She, in essence, said, "Lord, I'm not asking for the children's food; I'm asking for the scraps. I only need the leftovers to get my daughter healed." Her daughter was healed that same hour.

The woman with the issue of blood knew the Jewish law traditions and customs, but after spending all of her money, time, and energy without getting better but rather worse, she touched the hem of Jesus' clothing and was healed *(Luke 8:42–48).* When Jesus stopped in His tracks, asking, "Who touched Me?" the woman came to Jesus trembling, not just for fear but also in humble respect.

In the natural, anyone could have said they touched Him, but only one person could have said so in truth. Peter was correct, "Throngs of people are around You. Any number of people could have touched You. How can You even ask the question?" This touch was different from others. This was a touch of the humility of faith. This woman wasn't trying to be seen or discovered; she was only trying to be healed. Once discovered, she told her story. Jesus then told the woman, *"Daughter, be of good comfort: thy faith hath made thee whole…" (Luke 8:48, KJV)*

"For whosoever exalteth himself shall be abased; and he that humbleth himself shall be exalted" (Luke 14:11, KJV).

We can come to a humbling faith when we truly realize our need for God. This woman came to that point where she tried everything but with no success. All of her money was gone; her standing in her community may have been gone. What was left? Unlike some, the Lord only wants us to come. Forget about who you are and what you may have done or didn't do and just come. Jesus will make you whole.

True faith is rooted in and directed to God. It is also focused, appropriately aggressive, intelligent, tenacious, and humble. Faith becomes quite a bit easier when we look to God, knowing that He is faithful. He promised us that we could ask whatever we will, and it shall be given *(Luke 11:9).*

The humility of faith is unpretentious and will help us to see and sense the needs of God and others. It will also help us to defend and, when necessary, fight for others. It is vitally important that we walk in humility when having faith in God.

Action Plan 6: Be Humble

If my people, which are called by my name, shall humble themselves, and pray, and seek my face, and turn from their wicked ways; then will I hear from heaven, and will forgive their sin, and will heal their land. Second Chronicles 7:14 (KJV)

It is important that we walk in continual humility, not only when walking in faith but also as a way of life. The humility of faith isn't humility as defined by the world, "*Having or showing a modest or low estimate of one's own importance*." The humility of faith is being responsive to God, being reflexively obedient to God.

Walking in humility is a choice. Each of us chooses to or not to be humble. It's always better to humble ourselves rather than God humbling us. God needed to humble the children of Israel after leading them out of Egypt. They refused to obey Him by not crossing the Jordan River to enter the promised land. As a result, God told them to turn and travel in the wilderness for forty years.

Upon hearing that they were to traverse the wilderness for forty years, they decided to cross the Jordan River, now refusing to heed the warnings not to do so. The people of the land attacked them, killing many. God led the children of Israel into the wilderness, not just to punish them but also to humble them (*Deuteronomy 8:16*).

Walking in the Humility of Faith

It is important to do the following when committing to walking in the humility of faith:

1. *Become and remain in total obedience to God.* Learn to be sensitive to the will of God. Bring your life into perfect alignment with His Word.
2. *Don't be a rebel.* Humble yourself so that the Lord doesn't have to humble you. Gage your level of humility by how quickly you bring your life into conformity to what Scripture says. Don't rationalize your disobedience to Scripture or say they are not applicable. Don't say a verse doesn't really mean this or that or ask others what it means because you find it hard to do what it says, all of

which are indications of rebellion. Commit to doing what Scripture says, even if it is difficult.

3. *Practice obedience in your natural life and do so reflexively.* Make intentional efforts to quickly do what those in authority direct you to do. Do so without grumbling or complaining. Be reflexively obedient; by doing so, you will develop an automatic, natural tendency to obey.

4. *Do your best* whenever you are given a task.

VOLUME 2:

THE UNVEILING OF FAITH

SECTION 2:

THE MANIFESTATION OF FAITH

If faith is the evidence of things that are not seen, how can we know in the natural that faith is present?

Hope: The Key to Faith

"Now faith is the substance
"of things hoped for, the
"evidence of things not seen."
Hebrews 11:1 (KJV)

Why art thou cast down,
O my soul? And why art thou
disquieted within me? Hope thou
in God: for I shall yet praise
him, who is the health of my
countenance, and my God.
Psalm 42:11 (KJV)

CHAPTER 10:

THE HOPE OF FAITH

It is impractical to talk about faith without saying something about hope. Contrary to the belief of some, hope is key to faith. It can be said that hope is the spark that initiates and ignites faith.

Believe it or not, it is impractical, if not impossible, to have faith without hope. How can I say that with such certainty? Consider Hebrews 11:1 (KJV), *"Now faith is the substance of things hoped for, the evidence of things not seen."* This verse is the basis for my thesis.

According to Hebrews 11:1, faith has no practical purpose without hope. In fact, faith is the essential element of the thing being "hoped for." Faith has no reason to exist without there being something to hope for. To say it another way: Why have faith if there is nothing to hope for?

Hope gives meaning and purpose to faith; it gives rise to it. Hope becomes the fuel that faith needs to aggressively move forward, pushing toward the things being hoped for. Hope also keeps faith centered and focused, preventing vacillation. This results in us not being double-minded and wavery. Hope fuels tenaciousness, helping us not to give up during difficulties. What would faith be the substance of if there's nothing to hope for?

In the past, the faith movement rejected hope in an effort to achieve faith. That resulted in difficulty for believers to have faith, partly because the mere use of the word "hope" was frowned upon and secondly because the application of such a principle was confusing.

It was also confusing because if one was asked to define "faith," most would quote Hebrews 11:1 (KJV), "*Now faith is the substance of things 'hoped for' the evidence of things not seen.*" This meant that believers had to ignore or cancel out in their minds the word "hope." In the "Now Faith" arena, there was little to no place for hope. The Scriptures, however, say the opposite.

Hebrews 11:1 really says that faith must have hope to exist. If "*...faith is the substance of things 'hoped for...,'*" if one doesn't hope, there is no need for faith. Simply put, there has to be hope for faith to be the substance of that which is being hoped for.

Romans 5:5 (KJV) says, "*And hope maketh not ashamed...*" "Hope" there translates to "anticipate," usually with pleasure, expectation, or confidence. This describes a faith producing hope. A hope that increases as faith increases. Expectation is a part of hope; it comes with the package, and we cannot remain focused or tenaciously believe God without it.

It's okay to hope and to hope when having "F.A.I.T.H. in God." In fact, without hope in God, one cannot have faith in God.

One last thing about the believer's hope. The believer's hope is not based upon happenstance, luck, or any such thing. The believer's hope is not based upon his or her own ability to somehow work things out. The hope of the believer is and should always be in God.

Again, if we could do it, it would be done. We will always feel challenged in areas where our abilities are or seem to be exceeded. That's why each of our hope must be directed to and placed squarely in God. Believers must place their hope in God.

Hope in God is hope, and it's essential to faith. Never lose hope. If there's to be faith in God, there must be hope in God. No matter what you're facing or how difficult things may be or become, you must maintain your hope in God. Never allow your confidence in God to be shaken due to a lack of hope.

Hope is expectation. Expect God to do what you ask of Him. That assumes, however, that you are not asking for that which opposes His will. God is not obligated to do what is against His will. No matter what you see or what discouraging thing may take place, hope in God.

Hope expects God to heal, deliver, set free, supply needs, open doors that need to be opened, etc. No matter what, hope in God. Whatever confidence you have in God will eventually fail if you lose hope in Him. If you don't have hope in God, get it. Only you can place and keep your hope in God.

Remember, there can be no manifestation of faith without hope. There will be no manifestation of faith in God without hope in God. Hope in God.

CHAPTER 11:

CREATING HOPE

"Remember the word you gave me. Through it you gave me hope. This is my comfort in my misery: Your promise gave me a new life." Psalm 119:49–50 (GW)

I was a young lad, maybe ten or eleven years old; I can't remember exactly how old. My mom left home to run errands, leaving instructions for me to do chores. It wasn't long afterward I found my way to the back porch, which was about two feet or so above the ground.

Seeking to eliminate my boredom, if only for a few moments, I sought to fill my life with a bit of fun and excitement. Noticing a few sticks of bamboo on the ground, I decided that I would pole vault off the porch.

Using a length of bamboo, I began to vault from the porch to the ground. It was fun and exciting. I went higher and higher into the air, farther and farther away from the edge of the porch. A future Olympian was emerging. Jump after jump, higher and higher, farther and farther, I sliced through the air.

All was well with the world. But I lost sight of the clothesline stretching across my air space. Picking up my trusty pole after another glorious leap onto the ground, I decided that my next leap would be the highest and greatest of all. Returning to the porch, finding the perfect place for takeoff, I ran to the edge of the porch, planted my trusty pole into the ground, and leaped into the air, catching the clothesline perfectly under my neck, separating me from my pole, casting me unceremoniously onto the ground.

Crash landing solidly on my back, I felt as if every bit of air ejected out of my limped body. Lying flat on the ground gasping for air, I could see, I could think, but I could not move. Like a fish out of water, I longed for that which a second ago I took for granted: breath!

Life many times does similar things to each of us. One moment we're tending to our own business, doing our own thing, when suddenly life comes along and sucker punches us in the gut, knocking all of the wind out of us. That's what it's like when we lose hope.

Losing hope is life's punch in the gut; having all of the wind leave your faith, you're still alive but can't move. *It's like being dressed up with nowhere to go.* Losing hope is like being in *sort of an in-between place, that place between where you are and where you could, should, or want to be. If faith without works is dead, then faith without hope is being stalled in the middle of the road after running out of fuel.*

Hope is that sense of credible expectation that a desire will be realized. It's based upon one's belief in a person, place, or thing. For there to be hope, there must be tangible grounds for believing that one's desire will be realized.

Too often, we confuse or conflate wishing with hoping.

Wishing for a thing is significantly different than hoping for it. A wish requires nothing substantive. It doesn't even require a belief. A wish is little more than a thought. I guess one can say that it is a like-to-have thought with little to no emotional risk. If a wish comes true, great! If it doesn't come true—oh well. There is little to no motivation to do anything with a wish. A wish flows in the direction of the wind. A wish is supported only by the momentary thought that conceived it.

For the faithless, a wish is safe because it requires the one wishing to do nothing. To wish, one only needs the emotion, thought, or idea for a thing. The one that wishes for something to happen lives in the land of it could, not it will. As a result, if it doesn't, they lose nothing because they have nothing invested. There is nothing substantive in a wish, but there is and must be with hope. There is only one stage to a wish, the thought or idea; everything stops there; everything else is left to happenstance.

There has to be a migration from wishing to hoping in order for manifestation to take place. With a wish, there is no true desire or belief, but there is with hope.

Desire is the seed that produces hope. Simply put, no desire, no hope. That is why one never hopes for what they already have. There must first be a desire for that which will be hoped for to create hope. Desire produces an intensity that motivates one to act. The greater the desire, the greater the intensity, and the greater the motivation. Without desire, there is no hope. Without hope, there is no faith.

For hope to exist, there must be a foundational basis for it to do so. The creation of hope begins with a thought, idea, or want, but unlike a wish, it does not stop there. Those thoughts, ideas, or wants must grow in intensity to be transformed into a desire. That desire then becomes the seed of possibility that produces hope, but for it to become hope, it can't stop there. That seed of possibility continues to grow until it produces desire that transforms into hope.

Hope may begin with a desire, but it doesn't end there. If it does, it cannot be sustained and will eventually be lost. The seed of desire must also be fertilized by at least one belief. That belief will serve as the basis for hope. In addition, beliefs that are in agreement with the desire will nourish that hope. The more sound the belief, the stronger the hope, the firmer the faith. Yes, that does illustrate the relationship between hope and faith, but it doesn't stop there; the growth process must continue.

Note: If one's beliefs lose credibility or are called into question, it can undermine the belief itself. It is at that point that one begins to lose hope. If not stopped and reversed, continued undermining of belief will create doubts, which, if continued, will create unbelief. That unbelief unchecked will create a loss of hope and potentially hopelessness. Hope requires belief; it cannot exist for long without it. Again, the sounder the belief, the stronger the hope, and the greater the faith.

Belief differs from faith in that belief is based upon something tangible, while faith does not. There must be something tangible and credible for hope to exist and be sustained. If hope exists, there will always be something tangible and credible to cling to, wait for, and to be patient with. That tangible credibility will produce the beliefs that create the trust that serves as the basis for faith. Hence, that's why faith is the substance of things "hoped for."

Everything that hope is, faith is. The main difference between the two is that hope requires the tangible substance that belief brings, while faith moves beyond the belief of hope and creates a trust that will produce the confidence to achieve what cannot be seen through natural means.

Through the process previously outlined, our hope transforms itself into the faith that produces the manifestation of the things we hope for by motivating us to put forth actions necessary to produce the desired results.

Great faith requires strong, consistent, unwavering hope. Everything must have a foundation upon which to stand. Hope creates the foundation upon which faith stands.

As believers, the basis for our hope is the one and only true and living God. Believers believe in what God says about their situations and circumstances. That's why it's important to have faith in God. However, to have faith in God, one must believe God, not believe in God but believe God. To do so, one must consider what God has done, then conclude that He will do the same for them. Doing so builds the trust needed to believe God for what hasn't been done. That is the point in which we begin to walk in faith.

If you want to have a faith walk, you must place your hope and trust in God. You must then allow your trust in God to grow to the point where you will believe God to do what seems impossible.

Thought to Remember

Wishing begins and ends with a thought or idea and resides within the realm of the mind. Hope begins with a desire, then adds to the desire one or more beliefs that transform into faith.

The mind is designed to respond to events, situations, and circumstances. The stability needed to produce hope or faith cannot be realized in the mind. The heart, on the other hand, is designed to weigh the thoughts of the mind, events, situations, and circumstances, then respond in accordance to pre-established principles.

The mind can and will vacillate, but the heart is stable and sound. A desire is a product of the heart. It is the seed of life of the things for which we hope. Desires must be nourished and sustained by one or more beliefs. If it is done properly and consistently, those beliefs will produce the trust that produces the faith that yields the actions (works) that collectively result in the realization of the thing being hoped for.

There has to be something or someone to believe in for there to be hope. Faith is established when one's hope grows to the point where one trusts God to do the unseen, that which is necessary to receive the thing being hoped for. Faith is easy when we understand and employ that simple process.

Action Plan 7: Never Lose Hope

"For in thee, O LORD, do I hope: "thou wilt hear, O Lord my God." Psalm 38:15 (KJV)

To have faith in God, one must hope in God. It is important to do the following to create, maintain, and never lose hope in God:

1. *You must have a desire for that which you want.* A wish must grow into a want, and a want must increase in intensity until it becomes a desire. At that point, a belief must be added to the desire. To have hope, you must have something to believe for; therefore, there must be a desire. All hope starts with desire, but it is important that it does not stop with the desire. It is also important that the one with the desire believes that their desire will be

realized.

2. *You must believe.* Belief is different from faith in that belief is confidence based on something tangible, what is seen, heard, etc. Belief is always tied to the natural senses. Faith, on the other hand, goes beyond the natural senses to that which transcends the natural.

The confidence of faith is based on the spiritual, what God said about it. Faith leverages the confidence of belief to do and accomplish that which is not seen. So to have faith, you must believe, and if you are going to believe anything or anyone, believe God. If you believe God, you will have faith in God.

Believing is acceptance. Accept the fact that it was God that brought you out in the past, and you will have faith that He will do so in the future. Believe that God is the One that brought you out today; you will have faith that He will bring you out tomorrow. Belief that sees and accepts what God has done will produce faith that realizes what God is yet to do.

3. *Place your hope in God and keep it there.* It will be much easier to maintain hope if it is directed to God rather than a person, place, or thing.

Placing your hope in God narrows your focus, keeping it on God's ability and not happenstance. God is credible. We can confidently expect that God will do what He said He would do, and there is no one or nothing that can prevent Him from doing so. We may not always know when or how, but we can be certain that He will.

4. *Fill your hope with expectation.* Hope without expectation is, at best, false hope, and at worst, it is not hope at all. This doesn't have to be difficult, and it won't be if your

hope is centered upon the Lord and His credibility.

Centering your hope upon God is believing with confidence that God will do what He said and being confident that if what you want doesn't happen, then God must have a higher purpose, and you must subordinate your will to His.

Previously, I shared the story of Shadrach, Meshach, and Abednego, who were faced with such a scenario while responding to Nebuchadnezzar, king of Babylon. You may remember that the king threatened to cast them into a blazing furnace if they did not bow in worship to the idol that was cast in the king's image. The threat was simple, bow or burn. Shadrach, Meshach, and Abednego's response to the king was simple also, "We will not bow."

Look again at their response in the book of Daniel 3:17–18 (KJV), "*If it be so, our God whom we serve is able to deliver us from the burning fiery furnace, and he will deliver us out of thine hand, O king. But if not, be it known unto thee, O king, that we will not serve thy gods, nor worship the golden image which thou hast set up.*"

Those young men, who may have been in their teens at the time, did not want to be cast into a blazing furnace, but they were willing to be. Guess what: God did not prevent them from going into the "*burning fiery furnace*," but He was with them in the flames, and He also brought them through the flames.

We know today the rest of the story. Would the greater victory for God, Shadrach, Meshach, Abednego, Babylon, and for us today have been for the boys not to go into the furnace, or was it what God did to bring them through it? Obviously, it is what God did to bring them through.

Hope doesn't always eliminate the fear; it will not always stop the pain or embarrassments, but it will help you achieve the thing that matters the most, a keeping and strengthening of your relationship with God, which is the greater blessing.

5. *You must trust God.* Trust is credibility. If you do not believe God to be impeccably credible, you will not trust Him, and it will be difficult to have a sustaining hope that He will do what is in your best interest.

Hope in God is based upon what God has done. Faith in God is based upon what God can and will do. So have "faith in God."

Works: The Companion to Faith

Even so faith, if it hath not
works, is dead, being alone.
Yea, a man may say, Thou
hast faith, and I have works:
shew me thy faith without thy
works, and I will shew thee
my faith by my works.
James 2:17–18 (KJV)

CHAPTER 12:

THE WORKS OF FAITH

Works are key to seeing the manifestation of the things you are hoping for. It's important to remember that faith itself is invisible and cannot be seen, but works reveal faith's presence. This is why James wrote, "Show me your faith without your works, and I will show you my faith by my works" (James 2:18). We can say this another way: you can't prove that you have faith by doing nothing, but I can prove that I have faith by what I do.

There are those times when we do not see the manifestation of faith because we are not putting forth the actions necessary to reveal our faith. If that is the case, other than by God's grace, there will not be a manifestation of the things we're hoping for. History illustrates that such manifestations through grace will be the exception, not the rule.

Always keep in mind that things in the natural and spiritual realms are established through agreement. There must be works applied to move into agreement with faith for the manifestation to take place. Simply saying that you believe God is not enough. You must deploy the works that reflect that belief and establish what you are hoping for.

Consider the works of faith to be similar to baking a cake. Where does it start, and where does it end? It starts first with the desire for the cake, the thing you are hoping for. That desire then grows to the point where it becomes the motivation to get the recipe that will be used to bake the cake. Then, the ingredients listed in the recipe are gathered. Next, the equipment is gathered as needed to mix the ingredients. At the appropriate point, the oven is preheated in preparation for the cake. After mixing, the ingredients are transferred to the baking pan and placed in the preheated oven.

Once the cake is in the oven, the waiting begins. Experienced bakers know it takes time for the baking process to be completed. No matter how impatient one may be or how great the rush, it takes a given amount of time to complete the baking. You do your part, then leave the rest up to God; time and the skills brought to bear but are no longer needed. If you did your part properly, things will turn out right, and they will do so at the right time. Don't frustrate the process or yourself through impatience. Once you do your part, it's time to cease your labor. So it is when applying works to faith. There will always be something that you must do, but once you have done it, let God or others do theirs.

I was a newly minted teenager when I decided to bake a cake. I read the instructions, set the temperature of the oven, gathered and mixed the ingredients on the box, poured the mixture into the pan, placed it in the oven, and closed the oven door. After waiting a little while, I peeked through the glass in the oven door. I then opened the oven door to get a better look at my developing creation. I closed the door, then left, returning shortly to look again and again and again.

Finally, the time on the box was up, and my creation was finished. I open the door to find this beautiful, golden-brown marvel with a deep depression in the middle. I learned later that the cake had fallen due to my continual moving and medaling during the baking. I guess some things just need to be done in secret and away from prying eyes.

Inexperienced bakers sometimes frustrate the baking process and themselves through impatience. As I did, they constantly check to see whether it's ready, opening the oven door, etc., sometimes causing more harm than good.

We do the same when believing God for the things we hope for. Instead, we should determine what we are hoping for, believe (in context) what God said about it, do our part by employing the actions necessary, then leave the rest up to God.

When believing God for anything, always remember that the thing you are believing God for is the thing that you are hoping for; don't settle for second best. Determine what recipe is needed to produce the manifestation. Do your part, then leave the rest up to God.

As in baking, there may be many different recipes for the same cake; choose the one that best suits your needs. There may also be different approaches; choose the one that's best.

Rarely choose the easiest one; choose the best one. But how do you make the determination as to which is best? That part can be rather simple: ask the Lord. Always seek God's purpose, direction, and guidance. You will not go wrong when you do.

Seek God's Guidance

It is vitally important to always seek God's guidance in everything you do. This is especially critical in times of testing. Consider the guidance given to us in Proverbs 3:6 (KJV), "*In all thy ways acknowledge him, and he shall direct thy paths.*"

"Acknowledge" God, in this verse, is "*to know properly, to ascertain by seeing*" (Strong's Concordance). That means that you must see God. Meet with Him. Get His thinking on the issue, embrace, and follow it. This verse should be on the heart of every believer. "Acknowledge" here also means, among other things, "to comprehend, consider, and understand." Acknowledging the Lord is not merely informing Him as to what we want; it's also being informed by Him as to what we should do. It is also getting an understanding from God as to a variety of things related to what is to be done.

This is why the verse goes on to say, "*...He shall direct our paths.*" It is important to get an understanding as to the direction the Lord wants us to take. Getting God's directions first ensures that our actions are not contrary to His will.

When we get God's directions and know that we are doing what we're doing in accord with God's directions, we'll not have to worry about our confidence failing, that is, as long as we don't subordinate God's directions to what the situations and circumstances dictate. That's what Peter did while walking on water.

Jesus gave Peter the directive to come. Peter got out of the boat, stood on the water, and began to walk on water toward Jesus. He did well until his attention was redirected from Jesus onto the continuing winds and waves. Once that happened, he began to sink.

As soon as you determine the things hoped for, acknowledge the Lord. The Lord will direct your path through His Word, through divine inspiration, and through wise counsel. Seek out His recipe. When you receive God's directions, make sure you clearly understand them, then adhere strictly to them. Then, do not allow your attention to be redirected. Do not lose focus.

Do Your Part but in God's Timing

There is always something that we must do when achieving the things we hope for, but when we do whatever we do, it must be done in sync with God. When we seek God's directions, we are, in essence, partnering with God in order to accomplish the things we desire. Consider 1 Chronicles 14:9–17 to see why seeking God's direction is key to the works we must do while achieving the things we hope for.

And the Philistines came and spread themselves in the valley of Rephaim. And David enquired of God, saying, Shall I go up against the Philistines? and wilt thou deliver them into mine hand? And the LORD said unto him, go up; for I will deliver them into thine hand. So they came up to Baal-perazim; and David smote them there. Then David said, God hath broken in upon mine enemies by mine hand like the breaking forth of waters: therefore they called the name of that place Baal-perazim. And when they had left their gods there, David gave a commandment, and they were burned with fire. And the Philistines yet again spread themselves abroad in the valley. Therefore David enquired again of God; and God said unto him, Go not up after them; turn away from them, and come upon them over against the mulberry trees. And it shall be, when thou shalt hear a sound of going in the tops of the mulberry trees, that then thou shalt go out to battle: for God is gone forth before thee to smite the host of the Philistines. David therefore did as God commanded him: and they smote the host of the Philistines...
First Chronicles 14:9–16 (KJV)

In the above scriptures, David sought God's direction twice while fighting the same enemy in two different battles. In the first battle, God told David simply to go up and He would deliver his enemy into his hands. David went up as the Lord directed him and won a great victory.

David so angered the Philistines after their first defeat (maybe because he burned their idol gods) that they returned with additional help, determined to defeat him. David sought the Lord again, but this time the Lord told him to wait. I'm sure that David had the faith that he would defeat the Philistines; why then would God tell him to wait? The Scriptures tell us why: It was because of the timing of God. God told David that He was going to go "forth before him to smite the host of the Philistines."

Often, we mislead ourselves by thinking our victories are through our own efforts alone rather than by the Lord working with or through us. Much of the opposition we face is a result of spiritual influences. If the battle isn't fought and won in the spiritual realm, the struggles in the natural will persist.

Matthew 18:18 (KJV), *"Whatsoever ye shall bind on earth shall be bound in heaven: and whatsoever ye shall loose on earth shall be loosed in heaven."* It is likely that there is a spiritual battle raging while there is one taking place in the natural. We saw that in 1 Chronicles 14:14–15 when seemingly the Lord coordinated what was happening in the spiritual realm with that which was taking place in the natural. We see a similar example in Daniel chapter 10 when the answer to Daniel's prayers was held up for twenty-one days. What would have happened if Daniel stopped seeking his answer? We know that God can compensate and work things together for good, but should He when the situation can be totally different if we ask His directions?

We seek God when things are difficult, but when they are within our ability to handle them or we're assured of victory, it's easy to engage without acknowledging God. But we should acknowledge God, even when success seems assured. For many believers, that is the flaw in their approach to dealing with the situations and circumstances they face.

Too often, they use God as a tool to pick up only when needed. Such actions show a lack of trust (faith) in God, and they illustrate a profound weakness in the relationship that we should have with God. If we are one with God, where He goes, we go, what He does, we do, etc. We should continually seek the mind of God because we should be one with God and have a desire to remain at one with Him in everything, not just the big things but also the small things. True oneness with God will yield true faith in God.

It is important that we always seek God's directions. As stated in Proverbs 3:6, we must acknowledge, comprehend, consider, and understand what the Lord wants us to do prior to beginning our works. Acknowledging God is not just letting God know what we want and getting His directions; it is seeking the mind of God. We should seek God's mind in everything. No matter how easy the task, no matter how confident we are, seek the mind of God, acknowledge Him.

One last thing on the issue of acknowledging God: What do you do when there seems to be nothing you can do? If there is truly nothing you can do, there are still at least three things you can do: (1) Acknowledge God, (2) Wait on God, (3) Remain steady in your faith in God. As stated in Hebrews 10:23 (KJV), "*...hold fast the profession of our faith without wavering; (for he is faithful that promised).*" There is something about the thing that you are hoping for that sparked your hope. Continue to wait on the Lord.

Remain steady until the Lord brings about the manifestation.

Waiting, however, does not mean twiddling your thumbs. Waiting includes doing your part. Make sure that you do whatever you should do, when and how you should do it, then allow God to do His part. In the final analysis, faith without the corresponding action is dead. It's important that we do the things that we should do in order to see the things we are believing the Lord for come into fruition.

Action Plan 8: There Is Always Something that You Must Do

*"Ye see then how that by works a "man is justified, and not by faith only." (James 2:*24, KJV)

Like Abraham, if we believe God, the things that we do should reflect our beliefs. Abraham, through the things that he did (his works), established a deep, abiding, and personal relationship with God. God then gave Abraham directions; Abraham, without hesitation, followed them. As a result of Abraham's unwavering, reflexive obedience to God, he became someone that God called a friend. He was called a friend because of his relationship with God, and he always did what God told him to do. We that believe should follow Abraham's example.

The following are a few of the things that we can do to apply works to our faith:

1. Seek and follow God's direction.

2. Don't allow the circumstances or the situations to cause you to lose focus.

3. Don't stop. Do your part to receive the things you are hoping for, but do so in accordance with God's directions.

4. Do not procrastinate.

5. Do what you do well.

6. Be constantly patient once you have done your part.

7. Learn and get to know the mind of God.

8. Do nothing at cross purposes to God.

9. Always seek to accomplish God's will and let His will be your will.

Now Wait (The Art of Waiting)

Psalm 27:14 (KJV):

Wait on the LORD: be of good courage, and he shall strengthen thine heart: wait, I say, on the LORD.

Psalm 37:34 (KJV):

Wait on the LORD, and keep his way, and he shall exalt thee to inherit the land: when the wicked are cut off, thou shalt see it.

Proverbs 20:22 (KJV):

"Say not thou, I will recompense "evil; but wait on the LORD, "and he shall save thee."

CHAPTER 13:

NOW WAIT

Waiting many times can be one of the least desirable things we can do when facing insurmountable odds; it can, however, be key to our faith in God. So what should we do when we have done all that we know to do, and there's no change to our situation? What do we do when we have done all that is possible, and things not only don't change, they grow worse? We wait.

It is likely that there will come a time in each of our lives when we will face an obstacle, circumstance, or challenge that is far greater than we. What do we do in such situations? We wait. Not the disengaged waiting wherein one sits idly by in hopeless despair, expecting God to do what we should be doing ourselves. But rather the engaged waiting, expecting to see the manifestation of God's will.

I find great solace, strength, and confidence when reading the Psalms. David spent over half of his seventy years facing one challenge or another. From the struggles of youth, the plights of the shepherd boy, to the riggers of being king during some rather turbulent times. David discovered at a very young age what every person of faith must come to know: how to trust God. David, however, went much farther. David developed a relationship with God. Abraham also went beyond simply believing that God existed.

Abraham, David, and every person of great faith moved beyond merely believing that God exists and walked in obedience to God; they entered into a personal, intimate relationship with God. That is the key, not only to great faith but insurmountable faith.

The Relationship of Waiting

The key to insurmountable faith in God is a personal, familial relationship with God. Every born-again believer becomes a member of the family of God. It's difficult for many to understand that because they are so tuned to their own individuality and religious traditions. Such an understanding, however, plays a vital role in determining our faith response.

Every born-again believer is a part of the body of Christ Jesus, thereby becoming a part of the family of God. God is our Father and head of the family. As our Father, His desire may be to give us our desires, but His consideration must include how doing so will impact us and the family and His plans.

Most believers are so tuned into their wants and the religious idea of God that they find it difficult, if not impossible, to embrace or even fathom such a familial relationship with God. As a result, they never do the exceptional, and most never accomplish significant or great things in their lives. A personal, intimate familial relationship with God is key to doing the exceptional, and it is key to waiting on God.

"To wait" in the context of Psalm 20, 27, 37 is the Hebrew word *qavah* (kaw-vaw), meaning "the traditional delaying of action for a period of time," but it goes even further. *Qavah* also means "binding together," as in twisting or interweaving. That binding and twisting together creates a oneness with God that ties

God's will to our will and our will to God's will.

Qavah also means "to wait in patient expectation but to do so together (in oneness)." When we *qavah*, we do not wait alone; we wait with God; we are one. We are family.

When we wait in faith, we never wait apart from God. He is with us in every move we make. It's difficult to understand the importance of this without a deep, abiding familial relationship with God. *Qavah* lets us know that we are not and will not ever be "waiting" alone while having faith in God.

As born-again believers, we are family. We are not only waiting with and on God; we are waiting with and on each other. Why? Because we are family. What happens to one impacts and affects us all. That is the relationship of waiting. As we come into that, awareness, anxiety, and doubt leave, allowing faith in God to come to the fore.

There Is Always a Reason to Wait

Waiting on and with God not only means that God is with us while waiting, but it also means that God is waiting on something just as we are. There is always a purpose to and for waiting. Once we come to that understanding, we will be more patient while waiting.

God doesn't have a morbid desire to see us or anyone else suffer. He has no need to unnecessarily put us through things merely to teach us some punitive lesson. However, there are lessons to learn. Many times, the length of the wait and whether or not there is a period of waiting is a result of what the Lord must teach or bring us into the knowledge of.

There are also those times, as stated previously, when the timing and coordination of events between the spiritual and the natural must take place. David, Abraham, and others throughout history learned that lesson; we must also. If God is having us wait, there is a reason for our waiting.

Why Wait

When standing in faith, and after doing all that you can do, you have to wait. Know, however, that God will not waste your time or His. He will not unnecessarily take you through or hold back the things you need if there isn't a reason for doing so. That's why trust in God is so important.

So why wait? There is always a reason why we must wait for the things we hope for, but there isn't just one reason. Sometimes it is because of us; sometimes it's because of others, and sometimes it's a result of the need to accomplish the will of God. Sometimes the wait is as simple as the awesome mercies of God.

Noah took up to 120 years to build the ark. During that time, anyone that had a heart for God could have repented and stopped doing wickedly and started doing that which was right, but they did not. Even after the ark was completed, Noah entered the ark but left it open for seven days, allowing anyone with second thoughts to enter. The people of that day had up to not the last minute to change but to the last second. They, however, like many today, would not.

> *First Peter 3:20 (KJV), "Which sometime were disobedient, when once the longsuffering of God waited in the days of Noah, while the ark was a preparing, wherein few, that is, eight souls were*

saved by water."

Second Peter 3:9 (KJV), "The Lord is not slack concerning his promise, as some men count slackness; but is longsuffering to us-ward, not willing that any should perish, but that all should come to repentance."

So as we can see, as in the case of Noah, the waiting or the difficulties encountered while doing God's will may not be due to anything that has or has not been done; it may be due to the mercies of God.

To illustrate the extent of God's love and kindness, you should consider this additional side note: I think it would be safe to say that over 3000 years after the flood, God still sought to save those that were lost during the flood.

*"By which also he went and preached unto the spirits in prison" (1 Peter 3:*19, KJV).

One would think that after going through the flood, those during that day would have jumped at another opportunity to be saved. We don't know, but it is likely that many did not. After Jesus was crucified, many that had died previously walked the earth again for a brief time. Why were there not so many resurrected that there was a more noticeable number among those living during that time? Why wasn't there a *Walking Dead* type scenario seen? Obviously, this is conjecture on my part, but it does at least make me want to go *humm*.

Waiting is not only about us receiving the things we hope for, and the need to wait may not be due to anything we have or have not done. Waiting may be due to the will of God concerning us or others. That's why it is important to trust and believe God and accept God's will over our own.

God's Timing & Purpose

In addition to having to wait because of God's enormous grace and mercy, there're also times when we must wait because of God's timing and purpose. Scripture tells us that there is a *"...season and a time to every purpose under the heaven"* (Ecclesiastes 3:1, KJV). If that's true, and it is, should we expect God to be callous to the importance of timing when it involves the things that we want? I am sure to some such concerns don't matter. But they should.

Timing is critical for both God and us, but it's far more critical for us than for God. Remember God's instructions to David the second time he confronted the Philistine army? Wait. And do so until "*You hear the sound of a going in the tops of the mulberry trees…*" It was only then that God would go out ahead of him to give him the victory (2 Samuel 5:24).

Purpose is also critical for both God and mankind. It can also impact when we receive the things we're hoping for. An indication of this can be found in John 11 during the sickness and eventual death of Lazarus.

Lazarus' sisters, Mary and Martha, sent word to Jesus, informing Him that His friend Lazarus was sick. Jesus remained two additional days after receiving the word of Lazarus' condition. Before going, Jesus told His disciples that Lazarus' "*…sickness is not unto death, but for the glory of God, that the Son of God might be glorified thereby*" (John 11:4, KJV). It wasn't until the third day that Jesus finally decided to go.

I can imagine that Mary and Martha were very worried about their brother's condition and then devastated upon his death. Jesus, three days after receiving word of Lazarus' condition, told His disciples that Lazarus was now dead. Jesus then told the disciples that it was to their benefit that Lazarus had died. The benefit to His disciples and to us today was that God and Jesus would be glorified.

Raising Lazarus from the dead would elevate both the Father and the Son among men. Death for so long has been such a nemesis and formidable foe of mankind that raising Lazarus from the dead would increase the possibility for man's faith to grow tremendously, opening a world of possibilities. Such a miracle would also have a devastating impact on the princes of the darkness of this world but also upon the religious leaders of that day. In addition, this one miracle would do more than any other thing that Jesus did during His public ministry to set the stage for His crucifixion.

The religious leaders in Jesus' day enjoyed their life's station so much that they were willing to kill not only Jesus but also Lazarus. After Lazarus was raised from the dead, many of the Jews began to believe Jesus. Should such beliefs continue to grow, those religious leaders could not only lose their place, but it could also incite the ire of the Romans. To prevent such things from occurring, they began to plot the deaths of Jesus and Lazarus (John 11:44–53).

Where would we be today if Lazarus did not die and was buried for four days? Where would we be today if Lazarus not only died but raised from the dead when he did? If any of those things did not happen, the process of salvation could have been disrupted.

It may sound strange, but Lazarus' death may have been the most important strategic event related to our salvation, other than Jesus' death, burial, and resurrection. That one miracle put so many other events related to Jesus' crucifixion into motion (John 12:9–11). So, as seen in the events surrounding Lazarus' death, waiting is key to God's timing and purpose.

Waiting may not feel good during the process, but it could prove enormously rewarding in more ways than one. It's also why praying in harmony with God's will and oneness with Him is so important. God has not and does not obligate Himself to violate or subordinate His will to satisfy ours. Doing so can have eternally negative consequences. That may sound limiting as to what we can ask, but it is not.

It's Because of Us

Eliminate the *you, me, and us* factor. There are times when we ourselves are indeed the reason we must wait, and sometimes we're the reason for our own defeats. It is likely that that is the case more times than we think. So what do we do? Make every effort to not be your own hindrance to what you want God to do.

Anytime you believe God, do the following:

1. Take yourself out of the equation.
2. Make sure you are in the will of God. Doing so is the best way to ensure that you are out of the equation.
3. Be sure to do whatever you do in accord with God's word, written or otherwise.
4. Take the time to develop the discipline to do one to three. Too often, we fail because we want things to happen naturally. Such things are accomplished through employing personal discipline.

To get on the path of spiritual discipline, you have to read the Bible, meditate on it day and night, then allow God's Spirit to give you the understanding of what His Word is saying. Dietrich

Bonhoeffer developed a discipline of beginning each day with reading a small portion of scripture (maybe a verse or two or a chapter); then, he would meditate on that text for at least thirty to sixty minutes. Adopting such a practice helps to cement the study or reading in our heart.

In a world filled with challenges and so many things to do, you may never find the time to do what Bonhoeffer did and taught his students to do, but you can start. Maybe for you, it's not thirty to sixty minutes but one to five or five to ten, etc. The goal is to consistently do something. Begin the routine, then grow it into a discipline. This process will work for many things we do. It's how we learn.

Next, be filled and led by God's Spirit. Then, make a conscious decision to sacrifice for the Lord, doing so as long as it takes, even to death. Next, believe God and don't shrink from that belief.

After you remove yourself, remove the hindering people, places, and things that you are in agreement with. Agreements create enduring alliances; be careful as to with whom or what you form such agreements. This is especially true with interpersonal relationships. Rest assured that the devil will try his best to hinder or defeat you through the people and things you are attached to. They then will become things that you must overcome. Even in doing what is good, there will be things or people, intentionally or unintentionally, that can become hindrances that must be overcome. Remember, don't hinder yourself or aid in your own defeat. If you become your own hindrance or begin making choices that aid in your own defeat, moving forward will be very difficult, if not impossible.

Removing self-hindrances is tough to overcome for several reasons. They are difficult to identify and hard to address after they are identified. That difficulty exists because usually, we protect them. If, however, you want to move forward or stop putting yourself in such situations, how do you purge yourself of self-hindrances? First, you must bring every area of your life into strict alignment with God's Word. To do that, you have to stop living contrary to God's Word. Put an end to the justifications and excuse-making. Bring your entire life into obedience to the Lord.

Next, bring your thinking into conformity with God's thinking. Your sense of right and wrong has to be based upon His Word, not the standards of this world. Remember and employ 2 Corinthians 10:5 (KJV), "*Casting down imaginations, and every high thing that exalteth itself against the knowledge of God, and bringing into captivity every thought to the obedience of Christ.*" It's easy to instruct others to apply this verse, but it's difficult to apply it to your own life. Similar to what was shared earlier, anytime you believe, remove yourself out of the equation. To do that, you have to make sure you are in the will of God. To do that, you must make sure to do whatever you do in harmony with God's Word. Then be filled and be led by God's Spirit. From there, be willing to make conscious sacrifices for the Lord, doing so as long as it takes, even if necessary, unto death. Once those things are done, believe God, and do not shrink from that belief.

After getting yourself out of the way, you must also remove those that are in your life that are or will become a hindrance to you but do so in accordance with the will of God. If you do not, you may create even bigger problems. Getting rid of those whom you do not like or that frustrate you may not be the answer you need. Actually, they may be exactly what you need. It is important to measure yourself and them by the truth of God's Word, not your feelings.

People, places, and things can hinder our faith. It is much

easier to be careful beforehand as to whom you bring into your life and to what extent you do so. It is important that you choose your companions and relationships well. This is true, as it relates to interpersonal relationships but also true in business and other relationships. Learn to seek God's mind before making any choice, especially critical ones. Also use as a guide 2 Corinthians 6:14 (KJV), "*Be ye not unequally yoked together with unbelievers: for what fellowship hath righteousness with unrighteousness? and what communion hath light with darkness?*"

Never place yourself into agreements that pull you out of agreement with God. Agreements can lead to oneness; be careful as to whom you form them with. It's especially true with interpersonal and close relationships.

Binding yourself to those that do not share your commitment and devotion to Christ will, at some point, cause problems. It's best to be in a position of strength when it does. It will happen; it's unavoidable. An example of this can be seen in the story of Samson and the Philistine woman he wanted to marry.

Samson became betrothed, even having a wedding feast, during which he gave thirty men attending the feast a riddle to solve in exchange for thirty linen garments and thirty changes of clothes. This was a pricey wager in that day. If they didn't solve the riddle in seven days, Samson would do pretty well for himself, but if he lost, he wouldn't have the goods to pay the wager. No matter, he was certain of victory. In his mind, no one could possibly know the answer but he himself.

After three days, the thirty men concluded that they could not solve the riddle, and they too did not have the goods, nor did they want to pay the wager. Therefore, they threaten Samson's fiancé, forcing her to get the answers for them; if not, she and her family would be burned to death, so she pressed Samson until he gave her the answer. She then gave the men the answer to the riddle, which they used to solve the riddle on the seventh day. Samson then took thirty linen garments and thirty changes of clothes from other men of the city to pay off his wager.

The story ends with the men of the city giving Samson's espoused wife to his best man, going downhill from there for Samson. Eventually, Samson loses his anointing, his eyes, and his life, all resulting from entering into relationships with those that did not share his faith.

Those to whom we bind ourselves can be a blessing or hindrance to us. Relationships such as the ones Samson entered can easily be avoided. Samson could have simply listened to the counsel of his parents and stayed on track, but like so many, he rejected good counsel. There are attachments that are not so easily dealt with. An example of this can be seen in the marital relationship of Abraham and Sarah.

Abram (Abraham's name at the time) was seventy-five years old when God came to him and promised him that He would make him a father of many nations. There was one problem, however. His wife, Sarai (his wife's name at the time), was sixty-five years old and barren. Needless to say, Sarai wasn't a powerhouse of faith when Abram brought home the good news. The full story is found in Genesis chapters 12 through 21.

Twenty-five years passed before they realized the promise. During which time they vacillated, even using a servant to become a surrogate mother; in Sarai's mind, maybe that's what God meant. God always says what He means and means what He says. It's so important for those with you and around you to have faith in God while waiting on God.

All agreements are important, but none more than the agreements between spouses. When spouses are out of agreement, much is hindered, even their prayers: 1 Peter 3:7 (KJV) says, "... *as being heirs together of the grace of life; that your prayers be not hindered.*"

In addition to prayers being hindered, spouses that are divided forfeit one of the most powerful weapons they have in their arsenal that can be used to combat their enemies, be they natural or spiritual. That weapon can be used to accomplish great things when working together. That weapon is the principle of agreement.

> **Matthew 18:18–19 (KJV):**
>
> *Verily I say unto you, Whatsoever ye shall bind on earth shall be bound in heaven: and whatsoever ye shall loose on earth shall be loosed in heaven.*
>
> *Again I say unto you, That if two of you shall agree on earth as touching an thing that they shall ask, it shall be done for them of my Father which is in heaven.*

Purely due to the nature of natural relationships, it is very difficult to bring resolutions to disagreements. This is why it is so important to be obedient to God's Word and not place what we think or feel above doing so. In the final analysis, doing what God said will be all that matters. If you don't believe God, it is unlikely that you will obey God, especially when things become difficult or seemingly impossible.

Sarah eventually came to a place in her life where she believed God. Before coming to that place, Sarah laughed at God's promise, lied to an angel, and more before finally coming to a place of oneness in her heart with her husband and with God. Once she believed God, her womb opened, and she gave birth to her only child. We, too, must come to the place where we truly believe God. When we do, our actions will reflect that belief. Once we come to such a place in God, our faith struggle will cease as it did with Sara.

"Through faith also Sara herself received strength to conceive seed, and was delivered of a child when she was past age, because she judged him faithful who had promised." Hebrews 11:11 (KJV)

Waiting on God can be very time-consuming and frustrating, but it is important to wait and do so patiently. The consequences of not doing so may be much worse than the wait; in Abraham and Sarah's case, that surrogate (Hagar) gave birth to Ishmael. That one act possibly delayed the promise for up to fifteen years, and its residual effects are still being felt today. Much of today's conflict in the middle east is a consequence of that act of indiscretion.

Not Necessarily Your Fault

Hopefully, by now, you understand that there are many reasons why the things that we believe the Lord for are hindered, resulting in our having to wait for the things we may be hoping for. Sometimes, it's because of the timing and purpose of God, and sometimes, it's because of what we ourselves or someone else have done, are doing, or have not done.

There is one other thing we must be aware of that can cause us significant hindrances and waiting while believing the Lord. Spiritual hindrances. Hindrances caused by our adversary, the devil. Spiritual hindrances can be the most difficult to get rid of because we're usually unaware of them.

Usually, when spiritual hindrances occur, we're doing things as usual, but seemingly for no reason, things do not go as planned. Sometimes, no matter what we do, we just can't get the breakthroughs we need. We see an example of this when Daniel sought an answer from God, but evil influences hindered the answer from God for twenty-one days. On the twenty-fifth day, an angel from God came to Daniel with the answer he sought. The angel told Daniel that the prince of the kingdom of Persia held the message up. The angel went on to tell Daniel that he had to get back to assist in the battle. From this account, it's likely that Daniel's prayer wasn't the only prayer being hindered.

When this type of spiritual hindrance takes place, make sure that you and others are not the hindrance, then pray. You must then apply the principles set forth by Jesus in Matthew 18:18–19; do so while praying and even after praying. Remember binding on earth is more than simply saying, as some do, "I bind you, devil." Binding on earth begins by giving no place to the devil; to do that, you must walk in strict obedience to the Word of God.

There is more to binding and losing that I won't get into now, but it is important to understand that we must bind on earth so that the Lord can bind in heaven. Remember 1 Chronicles 14:15 (ESV), *"...when you hear the sound of marching in the tops of the balsam trees, then go out to battle, for God has gone out before you..."* Be mindful that there are battles going on in the spiritual realm impacting what happens in the natural realm. Those battles may have to be won to win the natural ones. The things you cause, you have the power to solve unless you set off an overwhelming, cascading event. For those, you will need help. That's why we must always acknowledge God.

The Perspective of Waiting

There's one additional thing that's necessary to keep in mind while going through the waiting process: preparation. Many times what we call waiting is what God calls preparation.

Waiting many times is a matter of perspective. As I shared before, there are times when we cause the delays, and there're times when we are not at fault. There are those times when the princes of the powers of the air hinder or hold up the answers to our prayers or cause things to not go as planned.

Daniel encountered such a phenomenon while seeking an answer from God; Abraham and Sarah took twenty-five years before receiving the promised child. Could there have been something else going on as well? When there are great, destiny-changing blessings, there is.

Back in the day, when using the old hand-operated well pumps, the operator would have to do what was called "prime the pump." To do so, the operator would pour water into the pump while pumping the pump's handle. Doing so would create suction, which is necessary for the water to be drawn by the pumping. There are those times when the Lord shares beforehand what He is going to do to prime our life's pump. Doing so creates anticipation, evoking responses from us and others necessary to position us to receive what He has promised. Genesis chapters 12 to 21, 50, and Exodus 1 to 3, 12 give us some insights into that process.

This is my premise: There are times when the Lord tells us or promises something, but the manifestations may be days, months, decades, or even centuries before they are realized. He does so based on who we are, our relationship with Him, our level of faith, etc.; it's His prerogative.

This is why I said earlier that the waiting might be a matter of perspective. We may call it waiting or think our faith is being tried, and to some extent, it may. We may say or feel a lot of things, but the question should be about what He wants, rather than the things that may be going through our minds. Keep in mind that God doesn't lead us through things unnecessarily. There is always a reason why we go through; to understand why, ask the Lord; He will give you the answer. You may not like the answer, but He will give it to you.

> *James 1:5 (KJV), "If any of you lack wisdom, let him ask of God, that giveth to all men liberally, and upbraideth not; and it shall be given him."*

Too often, we seek God for the answers we want, not the ones we need. Don't do that; it will lead you deeper into doubt. Believers should live unto the Lord, not themselves. The believer's goal should be to do the will of the Father, even unto death. Learn to allow His perspective to become yours.

In Genesis chapter 12, God gave Abram a promise, told him to leave his relatives, and to go to a place that He would show him. Abram obeyed and left for the land of Canaan at seventy-five years old, his wife Sarai being sixty-five years old. Today they would qualify for social security in the USA, but they were just starting their ministry.

> Genesis 12:5 (KJV), "*And Abram took Sarai his wife, and Lot his brother's son, and all their substance that they had gathered, and the souls that they had gotten in Haran; and they went forth to go into the land of Canaan; and into the land of Canaan they came.*"

When Abram got to Canaan, the Lord gave him the first

promise of a seed (Genesis 12:7), but twenty-five years, a son not of promise, two name changes, and a whole lot of other things took place before Abraham and Sarah received Isaac, the child God promised.

Then there was the promise of Abraham's seed going into another land that was not theirs, where they would be eventually ill-treated for 400 years, after which the Lord would bring them back into the land of promise to possess it (see Genesis 15:13, Exodus 1:8–10).

> *Now the sojourning of the children of Israel, who dwelt in Egypt, was four hundred and thirty years. And it came to pass at the end of the four hundred and thirty years, even the selfsame day it came to pass, that all the hosts of the LORD went out from the land of Egypt.*
> *Exodus 12:40–41 (KJV)*

I would imagine that the children of Israel were not enjoying those years of affliction God told Abraham about before they were even born. In Exodus chapter 3, Israel prayed fervently to God because of the harsh bondage and persecution they were under. Israel's perspective as to their plight was a bit different from God's perspective. Things may not have made sense to Israel, and today it may not make sense to us, but to God, it made perfect sense.

To Israel, they were simply trying to live their lives, but what was God accomplishing? We know a few things that God needed to do with Israel: They were going to be a nation, so they needed a population increase. They also needed to increase in wealth, talents, and skills. Most importantly, however, they were going to be a godly nation, so they would need a different relationship with God.

God sought to accomplish all of those things and more during Israel's time of waiting. That's another example as to why it is so important to have faith in God and to seek the mind of God. Confidence and not doubting is unlikely to get to where you need to be. Why? There are times when confidence will not change or affect the outcome.

So why does God tell us things that often get our hopes up, seemingly for nothing? First, God never gives us false hopes. It is against His nature to do so. Giving false hopes is never the case with God.

There are also times when God tells us things in advance, not to let us know what is about to happen but to let us know what *will* happen. Sometimes He informs us so that we can prepare for what is to come, sometimes to encourage us, and sometimes to build our faith to believe Him for even greater things.

"And now I have told you before it come to pass, that, when it is come to pass, ye might believe."
John 14:29 (KJV)

Waiting is a matter of perspective, which is why it is always wise to seek the mind of God while waiting.

Action Plan 9: Learn How to Wait on God

And therefore will the LORD wait, that he may be gracious unto you, and therefore will he be exalted, that he may have mercy upon you: for the LORD is a God of judgment: blessed are all they that wait for him.
Isaiah 30:18 (KJV):

But they that wait upon the LORD shall renew their strength; they shall mount up with wings as eagles; they shall run, and not be weary; and they shall walk, and not faint. Isaiah 40:31 (KJV)

Waiting can be one of the most difficult things that we do when we're in need or want. However, you can be assured that at some point in your life, you are going to have to wait on God. That wait will be much less difficult if you know the mind of God as it relates to our situation.

We can know the mind of God, but doing so starts with prayer and reading and learning His Word. The Bible is our glimpse into the mind of God. Creation (nature) is our first glimpse. If you do not have a desire to read the Bible, you don't have a desire to learn the mind of God or hear His voice.

People will say that they want to hear God speak to them, but at the same time, they will have little or no desire to read the Bible. If we refuse to hear what He has said in the Bible, what makes us think we are going to hear Him if He speaks audibly? God is one with His Word.

If you want to learn how to wait on the Lord in faith, do the following:

1. *Read the Bible.* Reading the Bible gives us insights into the mind of God and helps us to live lives that are pleasing to God.

2. Grow in your relationship with God.

3. Don't be slothful and lazy.

4. Allow God to show His mercy and grace to others, just

as He has to you.

5. Don't do anything to hinder God or to prolong the wait.
6. Remove any hindrances from your life and don't be a hindrance to others.
7. Help those close to you to believe God and to grow in faith.
8. Engage. Do whatever you need to do to facilitate the process.
9. Know that God has not forgotten you, nor has He forsaken you.
10. Don't lose faith and don't stop hoping. Never give up.

Trust in the Lord

Psalm 37:5 (KJV):

"Commit thy way unto The LORD;
"trust also in him; and he shall
"bring it to pass."

CHAPTER 14:

LEARN TO TRUST (IN THE LORD)

Trust. When it's all said and done, more than anything else, our faith comes down to how much we trust. How much do you really trust God? Not just trust in God but trust God the person. Your faith in God will be in direct correlation to your trust in God.

Many years ago, when I started my first business, I went to a bank for a small loan. I was about twenty-six years old at the time. I met with a loan officer who asked a series of questions, after which he stated, in essence, some people make good employees, but they don't always do as well when they start their own business. I went away without the loan.

The loan officer was really saying that he didn't trust me, not necessarily me as a person as much as my ability to succeed in business. Of course, the two can be one and the same.

I had no track record, so the banker was right; at the time, there was little in me in which to base his trust in me upon. I was buying a business that was failing, with no expertise as to how to turn it around. In fact, I knew nothing about the business I was buying. To make matters even worse, I didn't know anything about business. I was a young, energetic, inner-city boy, born in the projects who believed that if someone went into business, they automatically became rich. I was in for a rude awakening.

To acquire the business, I borrowed a total of twelve hundred dollars for the down payment on the purchase. Included in that amount was two hundred dollars; in my mind, I would have a big two hundred dollars remaining to get the business up and running. I was in for another rude awakening after finding out that I had to hire an attorney to transfer the ownership of the business and file documents. After paying everything, I had a big $2.65 left over to start the business.

I prayed, acknowledged the Lord in my way, believed that He would direct my path, placed that $2.65 in a cash box, and opened the door to my new business. At the time, I was about six years into my new life in Christ and was full of faith and zeal. My mantra was Philippians 4:13 (KJV), "*I can do all things through Christ which strengtheneth me.*" I was confident that I could succeed. I believed God. That was December of that year; by December of the following year, the business quadrupled, continuing its growth until I transitioned away from it into other ventures.

I believed that God was my source; I trusted Him and believed that I would succeed. I struggled greatly in that business, starting with no money; oh, not quite true; I had $2.65. My struggles were not a sign that I had no faith or that I had little faith; my struggles were an indication of the greatness of my faith. The struggles I faced were indications that I had faith in God. My faith is what kept me from giving up.

It was my faith that kept me believing God when things got really, really tough. It was my faith that kept me from cheating others and taking advantage of them, even while I was suffering a significant lack in my own life. It was my faith that helped me to adhere to the principles of God in spite of what I was feeling, seeing, and dealing with.

Too often, we think that our struggles are a sign of our lack of faith, but in reality, it is the opposite. Your struggles are a sign of your faith, not a lack of faith. Your struggles when believing in God are a sign that we haven't given up. Not giving up is a sign that you still believe God. The fact that you haven't given up is a sign that you are still resisting the devil and that you can go on. So don't ever give up or give in to that which is against God's will for your life.

Your willingness and tenacious determination to hang in there is a sign of your faith, not the lack of faith. That's what Jesus was telling Jairus to do, "Only believe"; don't give up. That is what He is telling us today, "Only believe"; don't give up.

Trying to succeed in that first business was exceedingly difficult, but I hung in there. I believed not in my abilities but in God's ability. I not only kept my faith in God, but I also grew in my faith in and my love for God. I learn to trust Him more. I grew closer to Him. Things became increasingly clearer; He was not only my God; He was my Father.

I then began to see the favor of God work in my life. Clients that left the business before I purchased it started coming back. Clients that did not leave began to buy more. I sensed they were trying to help me to succeed and succeed, I did. Later, I needed a vehicle for the business but still had no credit and no banking relationship. I went to another bank seeking a ninety-day loan; I spoke to the loan officer. Harold Pate was his name; he told me to come back a little later. When I returned, I filled out an application and walked away with a check to pay for the vehicle.

A few years later, I spoke with Harold asking him, "Harold, remember that loan you gave me a while ago?" He said, "Yes, I remember." I told him, "I would not have given myself that loan."

He said intently, "I knew you were going to repay it." Repay it I did; Harold was saying he trusted me. He had faith in me, and his actions followed.

The word "credit" means "trust or belief." In Latin, the word "credit" is derived from the word "credo," meaning "I trust in you." That is what faith in God is about, trusting in God; no matter how things look or how difficult or dire they may seem, trust God. Do not trust the circumstances or the situations; trust God. Do you trust God? What line of credit have you given God in your life? Is it limited or limitless? How much do you really trust God?

We don't realize it, but when we fear our circumstances and doubt God, we are placing more trust in the abilities of the circumstances than we're placing in the abilities of God. When we do that, we are really saying that we have faith in the circumstances but doubt God. There is no getting around having faith in God.

When I went into business, if I had allowed my lack of resources and support to get the best of me, I would have failed. If I had placed faith and confidence in my abilities and myself alone, I would have failed. If I had placed my confidence in others more than in the Lord, I would have failed. I had self-confidence, but my self-confidence was founded upon the Christ that was in me, not apart from me.

As recorded in Colossians 1:27, it was the Christ that was dwelling in me that was giving me the assurance that I could and would succeed. In everything you do, you must allow the Christ in you to do the same. You must extend God the credit that He needs to do the work that is needed to be done in your life and your life's situations.

Faith doesn't have to be a strange, elusive, difficult thing or practice in your life; it really can be easy to walk in faith. To do so, you have to simply remain focused on the Lord. No matter how hard or difficult things may become, trust God and wait patiently on Him. He will not let you down.

When you are struggling to achieve or while you are believing God, commit in your heart not to lose your confidence in God. Always remember that God has your best interest in mind. That means that the Lord is not going to willingly do or give you anything that is contrary to His will for your life. His will for us to always have His best.

Jeremiah 29:11 (KJV) is a great scripture of meditation, "For I know the thoughts that I think toward you, saith the LORD, thoughts of peace, and not of evil, to give you an expected end." In the English Standard Version (ESV), this scripture reads, "For I know the plans I have for you, declares the LORD, plans for wholeness and not for evil, to give you a future and a hope."

The Lord is always preparing and giving us His best. Do we really want anything less from Him? I don't think so. Because He seeks only to give us His best, there are those times when He has to prepare us to receive His best. God's need to prepare us to receive His best is another reason why we must learn to place impeccable trust in the Lord.

Faith will never be easy where there is limited or no trust in God. If you are struggling in the area of faith, ask yourself, *Where have I placed my trust?* Is it in the circumstances, or is it in God? Take the credit limit off of God. It's only then that you can truly have faith in God.

Action Plan 10: Trust the Lord

Psalm 37:3 (KJV):

"Trust in the LORD, and do good;
"so shalt thou dwell in the land,
"and verily thou shalt be fed."

Psalm 37:40 (KJV):

And the LORD shall help them,
and deliver them: he shall deliver
them from the wicked, and save
them, because they trust in him.

Faith is impossible without trust. When we do not place total trust in God, we will walk in fear; fear will bring us to doubt, which will undermine our confidence and set the stage for our eventual failure, but that is for the grace of God.

Below are a few things we can do to begin growing our trust in God. Do them and, as you grow in your trust relationship with God, add additional pointers and share them with others to help them to grow in their trust relationship with God. Doing so will allow the Lord to do great and notable things in your life.

1. Trust in God the person, consider Him trustworthy, not just that He will do what you ask.
2. Consider what God has done in the past to solidify your trust in Him. It may be something in your life or in someone else's, but looking back on it will help you believe for things in the present and the future.

3. Don't limit your trust in God. That means that you must allow your trust in God to grow, which means that you will have to see God move in greater ways in your life. That means that you will go through bigger, "badder," greater things. Don't worry, however; He will be there with you.

4. Obey God's word, be it in the Bible, given by a person, minister, etc., believe God's word. You will know when you do by your response.

5. Don't give up. Continuing in faith while lacking clarity is an indication of faith. If you see it, you don't need faith for it. Believe God regardless of what you see or don't see. What's important is that you trust God.

SECTION 3:

THE GRACE OF FAITH

God's Grace (The Power and Influence of Faith)

Many, if not most, Christians today, unfortunately, limit the grace of God to undeserved favor that leads to salvation. By doing so, they reduce God's grace to a type of serendipity, luck, or fate. God's grace is more than His favor extended to us; it is also His power invested in us.

Grace is the power of God extended to us to do whatever must be done to accomplish His will in our lives and the earth. The unmerited favor aspect of grace is applicable because we did nothing to earn or gain the power that God gives. We too often limit the utilization of that power to salvation; however, salvation is just one of the first manifestations and utilization of the power God gives us through grace.

Grace is God's power to do and accomplish His will. It is God's will that we be saved (delivered from sin), prosper, be healthy, healed, and have an eternally personal, intimate relationship with Him. It is through grace that we can enter into a personal, intimate relationship with God. It is through grace that we can get to know God and thereby develop trust in God. It is through grace that we believe and know that God can do more than we can ask or think.

It is through our relationship with God that our confidence in God grows to the point that we not only believe that God can but also that He will and that He will do so for us individually and collectively. Grace is truly the reason that we can have true, unwavering faith in God and be faithful unto death.

Thought to Ponder

We must trust God to do the work that needs to be done in our lives and in our life's situations.

CHAPTER 15:

THE GRACE OF FAITH
(IN THE MIDST OF STRUGGLE)

Grace. Not long ago, I was talking to a friend, Bruce Assaft, while traveling to a minister's meeting. Bruce is an accomplished writer and prophetic minister of the gospel that has been in full-time ministry for quite some time.

I asked Bruce, "How long did it take you to get beyond the struggle stage?" I continued, "When will the struggles end?" Without hesitation, he said, "The struggles never end." He continued by saying, in essence, "God gives us the grace to endure and go through the struggles." Bruce is correct. The power of God's love and grace endows us with the ability to face, confront, and go through the challenges that we face in our lives as believers.

The lesson for every believer to learn is that God's grace isn't a get out of hell free card. God's grace is His delegated authority and power to act and to access His provision. John Bevere says it this way, "*Grace is God's unmerited empowerment that gives us the ability to go beyond our natural ability...*"

The church was birthed through the womb of struggle and persecution. God, in His infinite, divine wisdom, has so ordained that we will be tried in the fire. But when we are, it is not to consume us; it is to purify us by revealing to us our heart. Through that process, God facilitates our preparation for the life and times that lie before us. But the most valuable thing that our struggles do is help us see God more clearly. Struggles can also help to cement our relationship with God.

God's grace guides us through the struggles while providing us with the sufficiencies needed to endure, the empowerment to overcome, and everything we need to come out victoriously.

No matter what you are facing at this time in your life, it is likely that you will have to face something greater in the future. God has obligated Himself to do His part to prepare you for that eventuality. The key to that preparation is trusting in Him on a greater level than you do presently.

God sees what we do not see, and He knows what we do not know. That's why we yield to Him and submit our will to His and subordinate our interest to His. That is a lesson that does not come naturally for most of us, but it is one that we all must learn.

As believers, we must learn that what we face may manifest itself in the natural realm, but spiritual forces underlay them. To be effective in confronting them, we must do so spiritually. We must also do so while not losing trust in God. At the same time, we must grow in our trust in God. That's why God's grace is so vital. Grace helps us realize that we are and should be capable of doing more, but there is a limit to our capabilities. Our capabilities can only be truly expanded through God's grace. Overconfidence in self blinds us to that fact.

> *For this thing I besought the Lord thrice, that it might depart from me. And he said unto me, My grace is sufficient for thee: for my strength is made perfect in weakness. Most gladly therefore will I rather glory in*

my infirmities, that the power of Christ may rest upon me. Second Corinthians 12:8–9 (KJV)

As Paul inferred in the previous verses, our ability to confront and go through seemingly insurmountable struggles comes down to one thing: the sufficiency of God's grace. If there is ever a time when we need to endure, God's grace will help us do so. If we need to plow through, God's grace will give us the ability to do just that, plow through. If we need to overcome, subdue, or conquer, God's grace will empower us to do so and more. God's grace empowers us to do what we want or need to do according to God's will and in every situation or circumstance we face.

The sufficiency of God's grace is another reason why a humble spirit is important for believers to have. As Paul explained, our successes and abilities can become as leaven in dough that puffs up. If we are not careful, we may begin to believe (consciously or unconsciously) that we have done the things that we do through our abilities only.

In a sense, it is our ability, but only due to God pouring His power into us. The powers that we have are God's power given to us in trust to be used to and for His glory and to accomplish His will.

Imagine that you gave money to a money manager to invest on your behalf. You may have given the manager the liberty to use your money to invest in any way he or she may want, but it is still your money. In addition, all of the returns on the investments of the manager are also yours, according to your agreement with the investor.

The manager may place the funds into his or her account and use it to make other investments, but it is still your money that he or she is using. You, however, and others empowered the manager to use your money. That is what God does in our lives. He gives us His ability and authority to act on His behalf. Any authority or ability that any believer has is God's authority and ability that they use to do the things that they do.

It is a result of God extending His grace to us that we have the power and authority to act. It is not that we have done anything to earn the use of His power; it is because He loves and trusts us enough to lend it to us. As we come into that knowledge and understanding, we also understand that we have no room or reason to boast.

When we are truly humble, we realize that our strength rests in God's abilities, not ours. As a result, we keep our ears tuned to the frequency of His guidance and direction. Humility of spirit is being sensitive and responsive to God. When we are humble, our focus is on pleasing God and doing His will, not our own.

This is also why humility is so important to faith. A humble spirit helps to properly utilize strength while at the same time being responsive to the will of God.

It may not seem like it, but today we traditionally use faith to please ourselves rather than God. We use faith to tackle our problems, believe God for answers to our prayers, etc. That in and of itself is okay, but increasingly it seems that we give comparatively little consideration to what God's will is for and in the situations we face.

Does God have a bigger plan for or in your present crisis or situation? Are you so focused on getting out that you cannot see why God needs you to stay in? Do you love and trust Him enough to stay in the midst of what you want to get out of? Either way, His grace is sufficient.

I was in a meeting with Pastor Getaneh Getaneh, founder of Watch & Pray International Ministry. Pastor Getaneh shared with us the story of the persecution of the church in Ethiopia that ensued after the communist took power. You should be able to find portions of Pastor Getaneh's testimony online.

Pastor Getaneh shared with us his testimony of being hung upside down in a small room when his persecutors began to pour boiling oil over his feet. The pain was unbearable, rising to the point where he asked God to take him home. He carries the testimony of his scars all over his body to this day.

After asking God to take him home, Pastor Getaneh said that he heard an audible voice that said, "Son, it's not time for you to come home. Tell these people who persecuted you how I love them dearly." He asked God, "God, how?" He said it was at that time that joy started bubbling from his belly. And with the fullness of joy, he shared with his persecutors John 3:16 (KJV), *"For God so loved the world that he gave His only begotten Son..."* After doing so, two of those persecuting him thought that he had lost his mind.

They then took Pastor Getaneh down and began interrogating him with multiple questions. He proclaimed to them that "The power of the gospel is the same yesterday, today, and forever." He said, "Who works for Peter? It works today." Later, two of Pastor Getaneh's persecutors gave their lives to Christ.

For Pastor Getaneh, for Paul, and for us today, God's grace is sufficient. His strength is made complete in our times of weakness. This is why it is so important that our faith rests exclusively in God, in being God confident, and not in self-confidence.

It is through God's grace that He bestows in our hearts the faith we need and use to endure more than we can even imagine. It is not us but God's empowerment of us to do of His good pleasure.

Grace helps us to use faith in a manner that pleases God. In the final analysis, that is what's most important: pleasing God. God's grace is indeed sufficient. His strength truly is made perfect and realized during our weaknesses. With that understanding, we can rejoice during the times of our greatest struggles.

It may sound strange, but we can see God's strength more clearly when we have exhausted our own strength. When you have exhausted your abilities, step aside so you can clearly see God's ability. If you do, you will grow by leaps and bounds in your faith in God. Never take God's grace for granted. Grace will likely be the difference between success and failure during situations you will undoubtedly face as you live this life. It will also be God's grace that will help you to stand in your faith in God.

CHAPTER 16:

THE PROPORTIONALITY OF GRACE

Proverbs 30:7–9 (KJV):

Two things have I required
of thee; deny me them
not before I die:
Remove far from me vanity
and lies: give me neither
poverty nor riches; feed me
with food convenient for me:
Lest I be full, and deny thee,
and say, Who is the LORD?
or lest I be poor, and steal,
and take the name of
my God in vain.

There is a proportionality to grace. Another way to say it is that grace literally rises to the occasion. For grace to be effective in accomplishing what it needs to accomplish, it must be appropriately applied. For grace to be sufficient, it must be appropriately allocated and applied to every situation and circumstance. There is always a proportionality to grace.

"Proportionality" means "corresponding in size or amount to something else" (Oxford Dictionary). The proportionality of grace was expressed through apostle Paul's writings. In Romans 5:20 (KJV), he wrote, "*Moreover the law entered, that the offence might abound. But where sin abounded, grace did much more abound…*" The first use of the word "abound" in that verse is the Greek word *pleonazo* (pleh-on-ad'-zo), meaning "to make or be more, i.e., increase…" The second use of the word "abound" in the verse is the Greek word *huperperisseuo* (hoop-er-per-is-syoo'-o), meaning "to superabound, to abound much more, exceeding."

Romans 5:20 illustrates the proportionality of God's grace, showing that no matter how much sin increases, grace super increases. Grace increases more and more. This is indeed awesome, and it shows God's love for all mankind. No matter what sin we commit or how long we have been engaged in doing so, grace rises to the occasion to compensate. Grace covers them all.

Grace covering sin isn't hiding or cloaking sin but rather eliminates the debt of sin through payment. It's like covering or paying for a meal at a restaurant or other debt covered by the payment. The amount of money paid, allocated, or put toward the bill is enough or more than enough to satisfy the debt. That is what Jesus did on our behalf. Jesus paid our sin debt. Jesus paid the bill, and He did it through grace.

Through grace, Jesus paid the bill for our salvation, *"Even when we were dead in sins, hath quickened us together with Christ, (by grace ye are saved)"* (Ephesians 2:5, KJV). With the same grace, Jesus paid the bill for our healing, "*... by whose stripes ye were healed*" (1 Peter 2:24, KJV). It was also through that same grace that Jesus became poor so that we could become rich, *"For ye know the grace of our Lord Jesus Christ, that, though he was rich,* *yet for your sakes he became poor, that ye through his poverty might be rich"* (2 Corinthians 8:9, KJV).

You see, there isn't more than one grace or different types of grace; it is the same grace proportionally and appropriately applied to different areas, needs, situations, and circumstances of our lives.

Proportionality of grace is not only important in dealing with sin; it's also important in everything we face during our walk with Christ, and it is key to having faith in God.

The grace of faith is having confidence that God has apportioned that which is necessary to accomplish in your life that which is needed to be accomplished when it needs to be accomplished.

There's one more thing I must say about the proportionality of grace: *we* have been given the power to apply it. There are things that God must do, but there are also things that we can, should, and must do. In fact, God expects and has indeed commissioned us to use His grace to effect His will in the earth and to change this world.

Consider the following scriptures:

Behold, I give unto you power to tread on serpents and scorpions, and over all the power of the enemy: and nothing shall by any means hurt you."
Luke 10:19 (KJV)

Verily I say unto you, Whatsoever ye shall bind on earth shall be bound in heaven: and whatsoever ye shall loose on earth shall be loosed in heaven."
Matthew 18:18 (KJV)

And these signs shall follow them that believe; In my name shall they cast out devils; they shall speak with new tongues;

They shall take up serpents; and if they drink any deadly thing, it shall not hurt them; they shall lay hands on the sick, and they shall recover.
Mark 16:17–18 (KJV)

"And he said unto me, My grace is sufficient for thee: for my strength is made perfect in weakness."
Second Corinthians 12:9 (KJV)

Believers today have an advantage that the early church did not have. They have a measure of God's Word compiled in a single book that we call the Bible. We have a unique ability to read and study God's Word like never before.

Today's believers have a vantage point that the early church didn't have. As a result, today's believers can put things together and draw conclusions that the early church could only have dreamed of. Could this be what God was telling Paul when He told him that His grace was sufficient? Was the Lord telling Paul in 2 Corinthians 12:9 that he already had what he needed to deal with the thorn in his flesh? Could it be that God was telling Paul that "You have My grace, now use it"?

Too often, believers fail to use the grace that God has given them to address the issues that confront them. God, through grace, has empowered us to deal with any issue that we may face. We simply need to apply the grace necessary to accomplish what needs to be done.

The task ahead for believers is to better understand God's

grace and how to apply it to the situations and circumstances of their lives. That's why faith in God is so important.

As believers develop their relationship with God and grow in Him, their faith in God will increase. As their faith in God increases and they become more aware of how God expresses His will, they will learn more about God's grace and become better practitioners of it.

When God gave believers power over all the powers of the enemy, He, by doing so, gave them the authority to utilize, administer, and proportion His grace. Such an action demonstrates God's faith in every believer; should it not fuel the believer's faith in God? If not, it should.

CHAPTER 17:

ONLY BELIEVE

Believe. Believing is different from having faith in that believing is evidence-based and that evidence must be past or present. To believe there must be a tangible basis for one's trust or confidence. Believing requires something to be spoken, heard, seen, or otherwise done in a manner that will engage or invoke one's natural senses. We can say that believing is inspired confidence produced by one or more of one's natural senses.

To believe, one uses something that has happened, then applies all or portions of that thing to a present situation or circumstance to reach a point of confidence. The level of confidence is tied directly to one's view of that past event. So to believe, one uses what has been experienced as a basis for their confidence in a present situation or circumstance.

Faith, on the other hand, does not require anything from the past. Faith is not evidence-based and does not require external inspiration or something done to invoke the senses. In fact, faith often will make no sense at all and often defy the senses. Faith will and should become the basis for one's confidence. The more one's confidence grows, the more faith will influence how one's natural senses respond to what is experienced.

I've always found it interesting that Revelation 21:8 included unbelievers among those cast into the lake of fire but not those that lack faith. Why? The answer is really simple when we look at it: God does not send people to hell for that which they cannot apply their natural senses. When in unbelief, one has to reject that which is perceivable by their natural senses.

There are no wasted words in the Bible. Each word and every letter comprising those words are important. Similarly, every word that we speak and that is spoken in our lives is also important. That's why it is so important to live, speak, and believe God's Word, applying it to everything that we do.

When Jesus tells us to only believe, He is saying, "Hold on to the evidence that you have concerning the things of God, what God has said, done, etc." Don't doubt it. Don't reject it. Don't cast off the evidence that God has given you; hold on to it. That little tidbit will be your life raft to float you to the manifestation of the things you are hoping for.

When Jesus was on the way to Jairus' house to heal Jairus' daughter, who was near death, someone from Jairus' house came to inform him that his daughter had died. As soon as Jesus heard the words spoken to Jairus, He told Jairus, "*Fear not: believe only, and she shall be made whole*" (Luke 8:50, KJV).

Don't fear, only believe; that was Jesus' message to Jairus at the point the circumstances illustrated that all was lost. It is also Jesus' message to us when the circumstances illustrate to us that all is lost. Don't fear, only believe.

It is likely that at some point in your life, you will find yourself between the proverbial rock and hard place. The place where there will seem to be no good choice or hope for a suitable outcome. So what do you do?

What do you do when it seems that there is no way out? When in the natural there are absolutely no options available to you, what do you do? What do you do when things are hopeless, or as in the case of Jairus, when the thing that you have been hoping for is lost, seemingly for good? The answer is two-fold: (1) don't allow yourself to fear, (2) only believe.

In order to do the first thing, not fear, you must do the second thing first: only believe. You must not stop believing the Lord. You have seen, read, heard of, or otherwise come into the knowledge of what God has done; now, you must "believe" He is no respecter of persons and will do it for you too. That is true faith in God and how belief and faith can work together for you to receive the things you're hoping for. You must keep your focus on the Lord and His ability and willing desire to not only do what you ask but exceed it.

Note that Jesus told Jairus, "Only believe." Far too often, we try to figure out how the Lord is going to do it, and in the process, we think or talk ourselves into a place of fear and unbelief. We move into unbelief because we are not able to figure things out. If we could figure it out, we would not be in the place where we have to believe the Lord because we would have solved the problem.

If Jairus had additional options, he would have taken them; my guess is that he had already exercised his options before coming to Jesus. By that measure, Jairus was operating in failure, and he now needed a big success. The only way Jairus was going to get the success he desperately needed was to do something that he hadn't done before: believe the Lord.

Like Jairus, when you find yourself in a no-win situation, you need to believe the Lord. Against all hope, you must hope in the Lord and not allow yourself to lose hope no matter what.

You then need to believe the Lord, not believe in the Lord but believe the Lord. Believe that He will do what He said. You must believe that He not only can but will do what you are asking Him. You must also believe that He will exceed, if necessary, your request in order to fully manifest in your life the things for which you are believing.

Jairus came to Jesus to ask Him to heal his daughter; he ended up needing her to be raised from the dead as well. Learn to allow the Lord to do His job. Learn to allow the Lord to do the exceptional in your life. Don't allow a perceived failure to prevent the Lord from bringing you into a place of absolute victory in your life. In the final analysis, it does not matter how He does it or how long it takes, as long as He does it and does so in a manner that comports with your best interest and His will.

Belief, the Key to Faith

There's one additional thing that I must share about believing. The key to faith is belief, not just any belief but belief in God. Hebrews 11:6 says (KJV), "*But without faith it is impossible to please him: for he that cometh to God must believe that he is, and that he is a rewarder of them that diligently seek him.*" The interesting thing here is that faith is key to believing, and believing is key to faith.

With faith in God, there is a oneness of sort between having faith and believing. I know some of this sounds confusing and somewhat contradictory, but it doesn't have to be. As stated before, the biggest difference between the two is belief is evidence-based, predicated upon what is seen, while faith is not. In fact, faith isn't needed when things are seen.

There are three keys that Hebrews 11:6 reveals concerning faith. They are: (1) You must believe that He (God) is; (2) You must believe that He (God) is a rewarder; (3) You must diligently seek Him. Let's look at this a little closer.

Key 1—God Is

Believe that God is. "To believe" here means "to entrust, extend trust, or give credit to." In this case, that credit, trust is extended to God. Do you really trust God? Do you trust God with your life's challenges? Doing so means that you commit them to Him, then do whatever He says concerning them. Believing, trusting, committing to God; none of that can be done if you don't believe that God exists. If you don't believe that God exists, in whom or what will you be trusting? God exists, and believing that He is present in your situations or circumstances is key to your faith in God. If the belief that God exists and is present hurdle is not crossed successfully, everything else will not matter.

Believing that "God is" illustrates the closeness between faith and belief. How so? You can't see God, but you must believe God exists. Faith is present because you can't see God. Belief is present by concluding that what *is* seen cannot exist without God, who is not seen; therefore, God must exist.

One morning, I came to my car and saw bird droppings on it, but I saw no bird. Did the bird not exist because I did not see it? The evidence left by the bird was proof of the bird's existence, just as creation is proof of God's existence.

God is the only being that is or that can possibly be self-existent. How can I say that with such certainty? It's simple. Nothing can come from something, but something cannot come from nothing.

There can only be one exception to that rule: God. God must be self-existent, which means that nothing and no one created Him.

God cannot be created. If someone or something created God, then who or what would really be the god, the God or the one or thing that created the God? The creator would be the true god; then who or what would be the creator of the creator? Now we can go around that circle endlessly. The only possible and logical conclusion is that a true God must be self-existent.

Now, unless everything that exists is gods, then everything that exists must have been created. So there must be a creator of everything. If there is a creator, then there must be a self-existent God that initiated the creation of all things. There must be a singular, one and only, true and living God. If that is the case, then *God is*.

> *"Through faith we understand that the worlds were framed by the word of God, so that things which are seen were not made of things which do appear" (Hebrews 11:3, KJV).*

Key 2—Believe That God Rewards

The second key is knowing without any shadow of a doubt that God will give you what you ask for in accordance with His will; it is to adhere to the rules that govern the receipt of the reward. There are rules that govern the receipt of all rewards. The same holds true for faith.

The word "rewarder" in the original Greek text means "one who pays wages, pays what is due, or gives the prize." The inference here is that the reward or prize is a result of something that has been done. It also infers that whatever was done was performed in accordance with the guidelines previously set. As a result, the reward was given.

Do you believe that God is a rewarder and will reward you? Do you believe that God will give you the prize that results from your efforts? For you, the prize is the thing you are asking for. Do you trust God to give you what you ask?

There's another thing to keep in mind about the reward: The rewarder must follow strict guidelines before releasing the reward. The guidelines for the prize (reward) depend on the competition.

Apostle Paul wrote in 1 Corinthians 9:24 (KJV), *"Know ye not that they which run in a race run all, but one received the prize? So, run, that ye may obtain."* Paul is saying if you are going to be rewarded the prize, run to qualify for the prize. Competitors are rewarded for success, not effort. Then, they are judged to ensure they meet the rules of the competition.

Compete well during the challenge, and you will not have to worry about your prize. Don't, however, expect to be rewarded for not competing. Far too many Christians only sign up for the competition, or they're only spectators, yet they want the gold. That won't happen. You must run to win.

This is not a competition where everyone is given a medal. Only the winner gets rewarded, and that reward is based upon how and where they finish. God is responsible for handing out the medals, and He has set the guidelines for receiving them. Read the rule book (the Bible) for the guidelines, then run to receive the prize.

"And this is the confidence that we have in him, that, if we ask any thing according to his will, he heareth us" (1 John 5:14, KJV).

Key 3—Diligently Seek the Lord

Do you diligently seek the Lord for what you are asking? Diligently seeking here refers to the manner in which we seek God. This type of seeking requires at least two things: First, proper motivation. What is your motive and focus for your seeking God? The focus of our seeking should be on God, not our desire. We should seek first His will, His way (manner of doing what we do), and His outcome.

Most of us only seek what we want, giving little regard to God's will or what *He* wants. We don't realize that when we do, we may hinder or halt what we seek. This may seem cruel, but God's obligation is to establish His will, not to check off things on our personal wish list. This is why it is so important that those that seek God's rewards first seek God's will. That is the standard we should use when seeking Him.

Diligently seeking God requires perseverance. Not perseverance to achieve what the seeker wants but what God wants. We must be relentless in seeking to establish God's will. We do so painstakingly, rigorously, tenaciously, zealously, and in such a manner in which we relentlessly seek to establish His will, not our own. This is why it is so important to believe Him and to enter into oneness with Him. When we do, we do so knowing that His commitment is to supply all of our needs.

One additional thing we must understand concerning believing being key to faith: Believing is also integral to our hope. Without some level of belief, hope will degrade into hopelessness. Hopelessness will usually yield failure because one will likely give up or not invest the efforts necessary to achieve what's being sought.

Remember Jesus told Jairus, "*Fear not: believe only...*" When standing in faith, always fear not and only believe. That is every person's hope of seeing manifested the thing being hoped for.

Action Plan 11: Believe

Mark 9:23 (KJV):

"...If thou canst believe, all things are
"possible to him that believeth."

Mark 9:24 (KJV):

And straightway the father of the
child cried out, and said with
tears, Lord, I believe; help
thou mine unbelief.

Mark 11:24 (KJV):

"...What things soever ye desire, when
"ye pray, believe that ye receive
"them, and ye shall have them."

One area in which we all can improve is belief in God. Not in believing that God exists but rather believing in God. Having unwavering confidence and trust in Him. Believing that God can, will, or has and that He will do it for you. The following are things that can be done to establish and strengthen your belief in the Lord:

1. *Only believe*. Keep your attention centered upon God and what you asked Him to do. Don't become distracted by the circumstances.

2. *Do not fear.* Don't breathe life into fear. You can control your fears; you give life to them. We gave birth to those fears through accepting the circumstances. When we accept the circumstances, we consummate a relationship with the circumstances that produce the conjoined twins of fear and doubt. Once those twins are birthed, we usually raise and nurture them as a parent does their children. That process will repeat itself if it is not stopped. You have the power to do so. Don't expect God to do it for you. He tells us to "fear not" because the choice is ours. We must abstain from the actions that produce the offspring of fear and doubt.

3. Don't accept the circumstances. Acknowledge their existence without embracing them, keeping your attention on what God said, not allowing your attention to be redirected.

4. Focus on God, not upon the circumstances. Focusing on God will not only help to maintain faith, but it will also increase faith. Looking at the circumstances will do the opposite.

5. Don't second-guess God. One of the strategies of the enemy is to get us to redirect our focus away from God by getting us to us replace God's guidance with our own. Don't do that. Yield your will to God's will, then seek to

fulfill His will, not your will. Such an action will thwart the plans of the enemy every time.

6. To keep your mind on God, you have to seek His directions and guidance, not your own. This will give you the directions that you need, all while keeping and directing your attention on the Lord and Him only.

7. Accept God as being credible. A lack of trust in God will open the door to fear. Ask yourself: Is God credible? Is God worthy of your trust? If your answers are yes, then give God your undying, unlimited trust and commitment, even if it kills you.

Always remember: If the devil can get you to focus on the circumstances, your life, what you will lose, etc., he will know that there is a way to get you to doubt, give up, and possibly, turn your back on God. Never give him that luxury. Never give him the luxury of setting up residence in your mind. He will always prove to be one of those tenants from hell.

Action Plan 12

Know ye that the LORD
he is God: it is he that hath
made us, and not we ourselves;
we are his people, and the
sheep of his pasture.
Psalm 100:3 (KJV)

Putting It Together

If you want to be a believer that will walk in faith and see yourself growing increasingly in faith, be sure to do the following:

1. *Faith in God is confidence not only that God can but that God will.* To get to that place, you will have to risk failure. You will know you have reached that place when you have absolute, unwavering trust in God, even if it means dying in the process.

I know literally dying because you trust God sounds radical and even extreme, but what is the alternative? Should you deny Him or give up on Him? If He cannot deny Himself, how can you validate doing so?

If you are not willing to actually die for Christ, you will give the devil an enormous place in your life. How? If you are not willing to lose everything and even your life, the devil then has to get you to the place where you don't want to lose what you don't want to lose, and you will give up on God.

When you get to that place where you are ready and willing to lose it all and give up all, you will find that your life will become a lot easier. That is when you will truly "have faith in God."

2. *Never consider your struggles to be evidence of your lack of faith*; they're really evidence of you still holding on to faith. If you had lost faith, you would not be struggling. The struggle is an indication that you are still in the fight. As long as you're struggling, you're fighting the good fight of faith, and you're having faith in God.

3. *Never use self-confidence as a substitute for faith in God.* Self-confidence may be confidence in self, but it is not confidence in God, and it will never produce faith in God. Self-confidence should always be based on one's confidence in God.

4. *Keep your sights on God, His promises, and the things*

you're hoping for. Stay focused on God. Don't give up on what you're believing God for unless it's contrary to His will for your life or others.

5. *Be bold and courageous.* Learn to become aggressive enough to seek out, establish, and maintain the will of God for your life, the life of others, and in the earth. We fight our good fight of faith to establish God's will, not our own.

6. *Don't be foolish, faint-hearted, or fearful.* Don't shy away from things because they have never been done. Sometimes God preserves opportunities. If God has preserved an opportunity for you, you have to bring it out of obscurity into the light of life.

7. *Seek God's face, His will, and His ways.* Let Christ's mind become your mind. Be led by the intelligence of the Holy Spirit, not your own. Become more knowledgeable and wiser in areas and ways you haven't before.

8. *Be tenacious.* Never give up on God or His promises. You will usually have to fight for what you are believing the Lord for. Prepare for the battles that you inevitably must fight.

9. *Be humble.* Become humble if you are not. Never see yourself as more than you are. Always remember that humility is an attribute of the heart, not the head. In fact, it's important to understand that whoever you are or whatever you may become is due to God's empowering grace in and upon your life. It is not of your doings or anyone else. Therefore, you are not beholding to anyone

but God. Never forget that.

Never give anyone or anything the trust that you should place in God. I am not telling you to not trust others. I am, however, saying that it is unwise to give others the trust that should be reserved only for God.

Trust God above all. Do not filter your trust in God through anyone or anything. If you place the trust that should be given to God in anything or anyone else other than God, you will have set yourself up for unnecessary challenge and failure.

Ultimate trust in God does not allow anything to stand between you and your trust in God. If you do and that thing fails, so will your trust in God. That is one of the key reasons we lose faith in God. It may also become the focus of the enemy's attacks. The devil can and will focus his attack on any person or thing that you place between you and God. He does do so in an effort to cause us to lose trust and, therefore, our faith in God. It is unwise to place yourself or anyone in such a position. The better approach is to place total trust in God, and then through your trust in God, trust God for the ones and things in your life. As a result, no matter what happens to the ones or things in your life, your trust and relationship with God remain intact. Doing so will offer the best hope and outcomes for those whom you love and that for which you care.

SECTION 4:

THE PERSONIFICATION OF FAITH

Bringing It All Together: How to Manifest Faith in Every Area of Your Life

CHAPTER 18:

PERSONIFICATION—WHAT IS IT?

Personification: the attribution of a personal nature or human characteristics to something nonhuman or the representation of an abstract quality in human form (Oxford Dictionary).

Although the above definition does not perfectly match the concept of the personification of faith, it does allude to it. Faith in the life of the believer must migrate from the abstract to the tangible. Faith has to become an integral part and reflection of the life of those that have accepted Christ into their lives. Faith must be reflected in everything they do.

The personification of faith is the process in which the believer's faith becomes a part of and a key factor in everything the believer does. The personification of faith is also reflecting God's will in and through the life of the believer. Additionally, the personification of faith is seeing the things hoped for come into reality.

The personification of faith is accomplished through aligning and bringing into agreement and oneness the believer's thoughts, hopes, dreams, and desires with God's. The results of doing so will be bringing into realization the perfect will, plan, and purpose of God. When faith is personified in a believer's life, it will be reflected in everything they say and do. The result of doing so will be that everything they do will be in accord with and reflection of the will, plan, and purpose of God.

So can faith be personified? It not only can; it must. The believer's faith in God reflects God's will in everything they do. This will mean adding works to faith, which also means that their faith will be reflected in everything they do. Faith in God is always expressed in what a believer does. James, in essence, said that the faith of the believer is always revealed in and through what they do (James 2:18). Faith cannot exist without corresponding action. It is those corresponding actions that reveal faith and indicate that faith is alive and well.

We give life to our faith. We are our faith's determination. Through our ability to choose, each person determines whether or not they will have faith. God gave us that ability through our individual will to choose. We can choose to believe or not. We can choose to hope or not. We can choose to have faith or not. Through our choosing to hope, we sow the seeds that produce our faith. We determine if our faith will exist.

Hope Gives Life to Our Faith

The thing that believers do not realize is that faith can come to life, and it can also die. We too often think that we either have faith or not. I submit to you that we can have faith and then let faith die. Faith lives only as long as there is something to hope for and is being hoped for. Then as that seed of faith grows, it produces the corresponding actions that are necessary to see those things being hoped for come into reality. This is why the scripture says that "*Faith is the substance of things hoped for, the evidence of things not seen*" (Hebrews 11:1, KJV).

Where there is no hope, there is no faith, and if faith does exist, it dies when hope ceases to exist. This is why it is so vitally important to hope and always hope in God. Faith will also die when the desires needed to bring hope into reality cease. It is our desires that produce our hope, and it is through our hope that our faith is produced. It is through our faith that we're motivated to put forth the corresponding actions necessary to realize our desired results. This is why James said, "*Even so faith, if it hath not works, is dead, being alone*" (James 2:17, KJV).

Again, faith can be alive, and faith can die. This is why it is so important that believers do not separate their belief in God from what they believe God for. First, doing so weakens faith. Next, doing so makes faith vulnerable through the possible lack of hope.

A part of the reason believers struggle with having faith is that they separate their faith in God into two faiths: One is a religious sort of Faith, and the other is a type of confidence needed to get what they want or need. Doing so weakens or kills true faith. Throughout Scripture, people of great faith never did that. Their faith in God always expressed itself through their relationship with God. We must do the same today if we are going to be people of great faith. Believers must choose to have a personal, intimate, familial relationship with God rather than the traditional religious approach to God that we have become accustomed to.

The Relationship of Faith

One of the biggest mistakes Christians make is considering Christianity to be a religion. It is not. What we call Christianity is a reflection of a familiar relationship with God. Breaking faith into a religious faith and a faith of confidence to get whatever we ask gives the devil great leverage in undermining the believer's hope and, therefore, their faith in God.

Religiously, believers relegate their faith to praising and worshiping God, coupling that, occasionally, with a feeble attempt to "live right" while trying to be the best person they can be so that when they die, they will go to heaven. Their second approach is to try as much as possible to not doubt that God will give them what they want when and how they want it. Instead of hoping for things, they wish for them. They believe that if they don't doubt, they will get whatever their heart desires. But if they don't believe hard enough, they won't get what they want, unless that is, God has pity on them and gives it to them anyway.

It sounds silly when stated that way, doesn't it? In fact, it is hardly any different than what pagans do in their efforts to please their gods. Such an approach is not really faith in God as much as it is faith in self. At best, it is self-confidence masked as faith and unlikely to produce extraordinary results.

Faith should not be bifurcated into two different faiths. Faith in God is and has always been one faith, and that faith is and has always been relational, not religious. It is simply having faith in God, believing that God will do precisely what He said that He would do.

It is much easier to believe that God will do what He said He would do than it is to believe Him separately for a healing, a car, for a this and a that, etc. It is much easier to simply believe that God will do what He said He would do; God will take care of the rest.

God said that He would supply all of your needs…then, if you have a need, have unwavering confidence in God that He will do what He said: supply that need. If God said to ask anything (according to His will) and it shall be given to you, ask! He will give it to you. Just be sure that what you are asking is in harmony with His will. If God said that if you delight yourself in Him, He will give you your heart's desire, then delight in Him, and He will do just that. You never have to doubt God. If God said it, He will do it; if He spoke it, He will bring it to pass.

Rarely, however, ask Him to do things out of their time and season; unless the circumstances warrant it, doing so will be outside of His will. To not do that, you must seek to know what He said that He would do, then do your part to not hinder Him. Now that is faith made easy.

"But my God shall supply all your need according to his riches in glory by Christ Jesus" (Philippians 4:19, KJV).

"Ask, and it shall be given you; seek, and ye shall find; knock, and it shall be opened unto you" (Matthew 7:7, KJV).

"And this is the confidence that we have in him, that, if we ask anything according to his will, he heareth us" (1 John 5:14, KJV).

"Delight thyself also in the LORD; and he shall give thee the desires of thine heart" (Psalm 37:4, KJV).

"God is not a man, that he should lie; neither the son of man, that he should repent: hath he said, and shall he not do it? Or hath he spoken, and shall he not make it good?" (Numbers 23:19, KJV)

The Goal of Every Believer Should Be to Be a Reflection of the Image and Likeness of Jesus Christ

"Beloved, now are we the sons of God, and it doth not yet appear what we shall be: but we know that, when he shall appear, we shall be like him; for we shall see him as he is. And every man that hath this hope in him purifieth himself, even as he is pure"
(1 John 3:2–3, KJV).

That we henceforth be no more children, tossed to and fro, and carried about with every wind of doctrine, by the sleight of men, and cunning craftiness, whereby they lie in wait to deceive; But speaking the truth in love, may grow up into him in all things, which is the head, even Christ. Ephesians 4:14–15 (KJV)

CHAPTER 19:

GIVE THANKS
(THE FAITH OF THANKSGIVING)

"Giving thanks always for all things unto God and the Father in the name of our Lord Jesus Christ" (Ephesians 5:20, KJV).

"In everything give thanks: for this is the will of God in Christ Jesus concerning you" (1 Thessalonians 5:18, KJV).

On June 7, 2011, CBS News broadcasted a segment on the power of forgiveness. They told the story of then fifty-nine-year-old Mary Johnson, whose twenty-year-old son, Laramiun, her only child, was murdered by then sixteen-year-old Oshea Israel. The segment began with Mary singing a little ditty over and over while ironing, "Thank You, Lord, thank You, Lord; I'm grateful for all You have done for me…"

It was 1993, during a gang-related altercation, when Mary's son was killed. The interesting thing about Mary is that after suffering such a great personal loss and tragedy, her faith in God brought her to the place where she not only forgave her son's murderer; she also befriended him and did so to the point of treating him almost as a son, even allowing him to become her next-door neighbor. The story doesn't stop there, however. Mary started an organization to support others in similar situations.

It's difficult to get to such a place as did Mary if you can't get to the place where you can see God in such situations. If we cannot see God during difficult situations, it will be near impossible to give Him thanks.

For many, if not most of us, giving God thanks is a near impossibility during times of hurt and difficulty. Doing so goes against our natural tendencies and is not what we are accustomed to. If we learn to do so, however, our lives in Christ and our relationship with Him overall will grow by leaps and bounds.

Giving thanks during life's challenges and difficulties reposition us from being on defense to offense, and we move from being the victim into the place of the victor. When we truly learn the power of giving thanks for and in all things, even our posture changes from one that is defensive to one that is offensive.

When we give the Lord thanks, we change the very manner in which we stand. We change our attitude, behavior, approach, our way of dealing with the things we are facing, and our overall consideration of them. Giving thanks does not, however, allow one to go on the offensive carnally, but rather it positions us to hear from God, and once we do, we can then act offensively under *His* directions. It is at that point that everything we do is and should be done by His Spirit, not by our might or abilities.

When we truly give the Lord thanks, we freely transfer what we possess or have in our possession to the Lord. To give is to hand over, to bestow. To thank is to express gratitude. The word "thanks" may also be used to indicate an act of allocation, or shall I say assignment. The assignment portion of this is interesting because it is within our power to assign. We can assign gratitude or blame; we determine which. If we assign blame, we remain on the defense. However, if we assign gratitude, we move to an offensive position.

If we are going to give thanks, we have to first decide two things: First, what we are thankful for, and secondly, we must determine to whom we will give or assign our thanks. In the context of the scriptures above and this writing, we give our thanks to God.

Believers should give God thanks for all things and in everything. That doesn't give a lot of wiggle room for not giving thanks to God no matter what. When we consider the things we go through and have to deal with, giving thanks can be very difficult and doesn't seem to comport with having and maintaining faith.

One of the most difficult things for us to do when we are in the midst of a challenge or hardship is to give thanks. Thanking God for what we perceive as bad is not only difficult; it is, for most, unnatural. Giving thanks while hurting or disappointed can be difficult, but it can also be the most powerful thing we can do when and while being challenged.

It seems antithetical to faith to give thanks when things do not turn out the way we want. The feeling for most would be that they would be thanking God for failure. But would that be the case? Giving thanks to God in and for all things is not antithetical to faith; it is a personification of our faith.

Throughout this book, we have instructed, as the Scriptures have directed us, to "have faith in God." Having faith in God is true faith. When we give thanks in the midst of the crisis, we are illustrating that our focus is on God, not the circumstances.

The key to understanding Ephesians 5:20 (KJV), "*Giving*

thanks always for all things unto God..." is understanding the word "for," which in this verse, in the Greek, is *huper* (hoop-er), meaning (among other things) "above, in (on) behalf of, beyond, over, on the part of, for the sake of, instead, etc." Giving thanks for all things does not mean necessarily giving thanks for the adverse situation or thing that happened or that may be happening. The scripture is saying that we must rise above and look beyond the situation and circumstances and give thanks to God. This must be done no matter what may be happening at the moment or what may have happened previously.

We should always give thanks to God in the midst of the crisis and in the midst of the circumstances, no matter what they are. Another way to put this is: instead of honoring the situations and circumstances by focusing on them and responding to them on their terms, focus on the Lord and what He is, may, and will be doing as a result of the crisis, situations, or circumstances. Do so by intentionally redirecting your focus from your hurt, pain, loss, tragedy, etc., to giving thanks to God. We can do so because we know that in spite of the situation and circumstances, He hasn't lost control; in fact, in our times of crisis, God is eager to bring to bear all of the necessary power to bring us into the victory we may need.

Giving thanks is not only important in the midst of the crisis or situation; it is essential to our faith. Giving thanks makes it near impossible to fear and doubt because it redirects our attention from what we are going through to God. In addition, giving thanks to God transfers the situations we face from earth to heaven, from the natural to the supernatural, and from our hands to God's hands. Our Father in heaven knows how to deliver; He knows how to set free; He knows how to recover and restore, etc. That's why we should give thanks for all things and in all things. When we give thanks to God, we illustrate and resoundingly declare through our thanksgiving our faith in God.

There is one additional thing we must emphasize when we give God thanks: Giving thanks is not making a statement from the head and lips that "I thank You, God, for this or that," while your attention remains on the situation and circumstances. True thanksgiving, in all cases, is from the heart, not the head. Giving thanks is a reflection of what is in our hearts. For there to be thanksgiving in our heart, there must be a reason for it, and that reason must be based totally on God, not ourselves. To do that type of thanksgiving:

1. *Realize and embrace the fact that God does not have our limitations.*

Romans 4:17 (KJV), "...even God, who quickeneth the dead, and calleth those things which be not as though they were."

*Ephesians 3:*20 (KJV), *"Now unto him that is able to do exceeding abundantly above all that we ask or think, according to the power that worketh in us."*

The only limitation that God has in dealing with the situations and circumstances we face are the ones we place upon Him. We must remove those limitations.

2. *Transfer the situation from you to Him.*

First Peter 5:7 (KJV), *"Casting all your care upon him; for he careth for you."*

Always remember that God is not a thief. He is not going to take by force what we do not give Him willingly. "To cast" here in Greek means "to throw upon." Imagine you are taking some hot potatoes out of the oven. Do you hold them in your hand and bemoan the fact that they are burning you? Or do you hurriedly place them onto a plate or pan that the heat will not affect? Obviously, the latter. We should do the same with the Lord.

The Lord is the One that can handle what we can't. In doing so, He will strengthen us to do and bear that which we must. That is why we throw our concerns on the Lord. He cares for us, and He is concerned about the situations and circumstances we face.

I am not telling anyone to not care or grieve, but I am saying that there are ways to face the challenge as a victor instead of a victim. Just know that our adversary, the devil, if he can, will use every situation and circumstance to his advantage. If possible, he'll do so to your detriment. Giving God genuine thanks will spoil his efforts.

3. *Don't waver or hesitate to give God thanks in all things. Hebrews 10:23 (KJV), "Let us hold fast the profession of our faith without wavering; (for he is faithful that promise)."* Know that God is faithful; He can be counted on. Giving God thanks shows where we have placed our faith during some of the most difficult times we face. We direct our thanks to God because our faith is in Him, not in ourselves or anyone else. Our faith is and should always be in God.

4. *Get moving. Philippians 3:13–14 (KJV), "...this one thing I do, forgetting those things which are behind, and reaching forth unto those things which are before, I press toward the mark for the prize of the high calling of God in Christ Jesus."*

After casting our cares on the Lord and giving thanks, we must begin the process of moving on. This is where it becomes difficult for some, but we must move on. It's important to move on and do so as soon as possible.

The longer we stay put, the more vulnerable we become, and the longer it takes us to get back on our road to destiny. This is why faith in God is so important. Our confidence in God is critically important to the process of moving on; it may not be easy, but it is what we must do to continue the process of living the victorious life that the Lord has ordained for each of us.

It is important to realize that it's difficult to achieve victory while on defense; it's possible but unlikely. Our victory will likely be achieved while on the offensive. That's why it is crucial that we start moving as soon as possible.

CHAPTER 20:

THANK HIM FOR THIS?

"Giving thanks always for all things unto God and the Father "in the name of our Lord Jesus Christ."
Ephesians 5:20 (KJV)

Yes, thank Him for this, thank Him for that, and thank Him for everything. In fact, as believers, we must come to the place where we can freely and easily thank the Lord for all things, no matter what those things are. No matter how devastating the events or how pleasingly exciting they may be, we should always give thanks to the Lord for them.

As stated before, when we give God thanks, we are not in some morbid way thanking Him for whatever horrific thing that has befallen us. We're giving thanks in spite of what has befallen us. When the scripture says in 1 Thessalonians 5:18 (KJV), "*In everything give thanks: for this is the will of God in Christ Jesus concerning you,*" the scripture is not saying that the things happening to you are God's will, but rather it's God's will to give thanks, even though you are going through the thing you may be going through.

Giving thanks always for all things is to look beyond or through what you're facing to see God, His will, His doings, His abilities, etc. That's what the Lord was telling Paul in 2 Corinthians 12:9 (KJV), "*...My grace is sufficient for thee: for my strength is made* *perfect in weakness*." The Lord was telling Paul, in essence, "Paul, look beyond what you're going through and see Me. Realize and apply My strength; it is what you need and all you need."

Like the apostle Paul, if we focus less on the obstacles and challenges we face, we will be better able to see and apply God's strength. It is when we are at our weakest that God's strength is most clearly seen. In fact, God's presence and strength are most pronounced when we are at our weakest. When we think we are at our best, our abilities too often shroud God's abilities, making it impossible for us to see Him at work. That's not to say that we stay weak to see Him; no, we become one with Him, allowing His strength to become ours.

He is always there for us. He never leaves or forsakes us. In weakness or strength, good times or bad, our heavenly Father is always there. It's when we reach the limits of our abilities that He is most clearly seen in our lives and our life's situations. For us, He is always there. Knowing that and trusting Him, we can truly thank Him for all things. Doing so helps us to have and maintain our faith in God.

CHAPTER 21:

THANK HIM IN THIS?

First Thessalonians 5:18 (KJV), *"In everything*
"give thanks: for this is the will of
"God in Christ Jesus concerning you."

Thank the Lord in this? Yes. Just as in thanking the Lord *for* all things, we must also thank the Lord *in* everything, be they good or not so good.

While we are in the midst of the situations and circumstances we find ourselves, we should always give God thanks. We should give God thanks not only after we come out of the situations and circumstances but also while being yet within them. It is our faith in God that will empower us to do so.

If we trust and believe God, we will have faith in God that He has a divine purpose for us. We will also believe that He will work whatever we're facing together with other things for our good. We should also have that same confidence when we're where we are due to our own actions. From time to time, we'll miss the mark. Scripture instructs us to pray without ceasing and to pray and not faint. One of the easiest prayers we can pray during challenging times is the prayer of thanksgiving. As shared in 1 Thessalonians 5:18, believers not only should thank the Lord for all things, but they should also give Him thanks *in* all things. We can do so only if we have faith in God.

Our faith in God should be rooted in our assurance in God, knowing within our hearts that God can and will. Not necessarily that He will do what we want but do what He knows is best. Those who trust God, trust God. It is our trust that enables us to endure disappointments and helps us to believe God for more.

It is our trust in God that helps us to redirect our focus from ourselves and the circumstances that we face onto Him. In the midst of the challenge, in the midst of the turmoil, in the midst of the travail, along life's unchartered paths, we trust and learn to trust *Him*. We learn to have faith in God.

It is in our darkest moments that we can see (if we look) that His grace is truly sufficient. It's also in those times that we can (if we look) see His strength. His strength to deliver, keep, preserve, sustain, conquer, or manifest Himself in whatever way we need Him to (2 Corinthians 2:9).

We could see this in the life of Moses when challenged by the wrath of Pharaoh, with seemingly nowhere to go. To those he was leading, the situation was hopeless; Moses, however, turned to God. Moses had an angry, ruthless Pharaoh emerging from behind while at the same time being confronted by the people he was leading. They even threatened to stone him, and to top those things off, he was flanked by desert wilderness and the Red Sea before him. What did Moses do? In the final analysis, he trusted God. That is what we must do. Moses looked to the only One that had the power, ability, and willingness to bring the deliverances he and the people needed on all of those levels, and he needed it *now*. What did he do? He had faith in God.

Peter and the other disciples were in a ship being battered by furious winds and rains when they looked and saw what they thought was a ghost, which compounded their fears. Jesus shouted to them to not be afraid because it was He. Peter shouted back, saying, "If it is You, let me come to You on the water." Jesus said come.

Peter then used his faith and trust in Jesus to walk on water. Even when he took his eyes off the Lord, placing them squarely on the circumstances, the Lord was there to keep him from drowning. Peter called for the Lord's help, and it was there. Like Peter, we can trust Him even in failure, and He will come through.

One of my dear sons in the Lord wanted to pursue a new career that motivated him to move from the East Coast to the West Coast, to California, USA. He left a place where he had lots of friends and family to a place where he had none. He had enough money to get started and to sustain himself until he became established in his new city. He also set aside enough funds to return home should he not succeed in his transition. He stepped out on faith, believing the Lord would open doors for him.

After some time had passed, with no success or movement toward his new career and not being able to get a job, he began to wonder if he had made a foolish move. What that young man did then was an amazing act of faith. He eliminated his plan "B." He gathered all of the money he was keeping to get back home, placed it in an envelope, got on a city bus, traveled to a predetermined location, and got off the bus, intentionally leaving the envelope on the seat of the bus with the money in it.

He intentionally placed himself in a position where he had no one that he could trust but God. He was afraid; he didn't know what he would do when he could not pay the lease on his apartment or when the small amount of cash he had left would be depleted. In a relatively few days, he could be homeless and hungry. But God…

God showed Himself strong in that young man's life. David

said, "*I have been young, and now am old; yet have I not seen the righteous forsaken, nor his seed begging bread*" (Psalm 37:25, KJV). God did honor His Word and His promise to that young man. He was not forsaken, nor did he have to beg for bread. God will also do the same thing for you and for all that believe in Him. God's grace was indeed sufficient for that young man. God's strength was made complete in his weakness. God opened doors for him; he got a job and is doing well.

It's all about our faith in God, our belief that God can be trusted to do what He said He would do. Because of our blessed assurance in God, we can truly have faith in God and exercise that faith in God to do great and mighty things.

CHAPTER 22:

WHOSE WILL?

First Thessalonians 5:18 (KJV), *"In everything "give thanks: for this is the will of "God in Christ Jesus concerning you."*

There's something else we must consider that's found in 1 Thessalonians 5:18 (KJV), "*...for this is the will of God in Christ Jesus concerning you.*" The will of God? Yes. To truly have faith in God, one must be willing to subordinate and submit his or her will to the will of God. How can a person truly have faith in God and, at the same time, *not* be in true submission to God?

Far too often, we seek to use faith as a master key to get entry to and possession of whatever we want, when and how we want it. That is not faith in God but an effort to establish one's own will. True faith in God will use that master key not to get what "I want" but rather what *He* wants.

The will of God must be of the utmost importance for us to truly have faith in God. That means that we must subordinate our will to His will. It also means that our will must be secondary to God's will in all things and at all times. Additionally, we must literally lay down our will at His feet and take up His will as our own. His will must become our will. That's what Jesus was illustrating at Gethsemane.

Jesus knew that He was about to be delivered into the hands of men; the high priest would judge Him falsely and turn Him over to Pontius Pilate. He knew that Pilate would sentence Him to death and turn Him over to the executioners. He knew that he was about to undergo a period of extreme suffering. He knew that in addition to crucifixion, He was about to experience something he had never experienced, separation from His heavenly Father.

It is accepted that Jesus was thirty-three years old at the time of His death. It is also likely that He had probably seen numerous crucifixions before Gethsemane. He knew what a crucifixion was, and He knew the pain, agony, embarrassment, and humiliation He was about to experience.

Jesus knew the horrific death He was about to experience, not because of anything wrong that He had done, but in the minds of others, He had to be gotten rid of. However, in Jesus' mind, He was about to become the only sacrifice that could become the viable scapegoat that could take upon the sins of the world, including the sins of the ones who had a hand in His execution. Jesus also knew that taking on sin would result in His separation from His heavenly Father.

At Gethsemane, Jesus knew that if ever there was a time to pray, that time was now, and pray, He did. He prayed like never before. We don't know all that He prayed, but we do know, unlike any other time recorded in Scripture, Jesus prayed for Himself and asked His disciples to enter into prayer with Him.

Jesus knew that He was about to be delivered over to His persecutors. He knew He had to pray and that His disciples needed to pray with Him. So He also asked His disciples to pray. If nothing else, they needed to pray that they would not fall into temptation.

We know the story: while Jesus prayed, the disciples slept. Why? Because they were sleepy. That's the story, but I say they slept because, like us, they did not realize the urgency of the hour. Jesus, however, did and prayed. His prayer reflected the urgency of the hour. The Scripture records that He prayed to the point that His sweat was as drops of blood. In a time like that, for what did Jesus pray? If you were in Jesus' sandals, for what would *you* pray?

Scripture records that Jesus prayed, *"O my Father if it be possible, let this cup pass from me: nevertheless not as I will, but as thou wilt"* (*Matthew 26:39, KJV*). Some believe that Jesus was praying to escape the impending scourging and horrific death of crucifixion. Some referenced the suffering He was about to endure. All of that could be true, but I believe there was something else that was of greater concern to Jesus: His pending separation from the Father.

Jesus spoke many times about what He was going to suffer at the hands of the Jews, but He never discussed His separation from the Father. At Gethsemane, however, He knew that He was about to confront that very reality. It was something He had never faced in all of His eternal existence: separation from His Father. Now at Gethsemane, He knew that in a relatively few short hours, He was about to experience that very thing, separation from His heavenly Father, separation from God.

Interestingly, Jesus never prayed a prayer that elevated His will above the will of His Father. There is also no indication that He even had a desire to do so. Jesus only sorted to do the will of His Father. The reason for that is that Jesus' will and the Father's will are the same. That is true oneness, and it is truly having faith in God.

Faith requires each of us to follow Jesus' example. In times of our most difficult challenge, we must, without question, put God's will above our own. Always remember one thing, the devil's chief goal in every challenge is to get the believer to reject God.

When we reject God's will, we reject God. When we sin, we reject God. Always remember that God, His will, and His word are all one and the same. When we reject God's word or will, we reject God; that means that we can't be walking in faith. There can't be faith in God and rejection of God at the same time.

There simply cannot be true faith in God when there is a clash of God's will and ours. The key to having consistent faith in God is entering into true oneness with God. There will always be room for division or room to divide where there is a lack of oneness.

A lack of oneness is always an indication of a lack of agreement. When there is no agreement, it is difficult, if not impossible, to establish the thing being "*hoped for*." This is partly why we struggle in life and many times why we struggle in our faith. True faith in God is faith that seeks to establish God's will. To do that, we must come to an understanding of what the will of God is. When we do, we will know how to better direct our faith in God.

CHAPTER 23:

THE WILL OF GOD

"Wherefore be ye not unwise, "but understanding what the "will of the Lord is." (Ephesians 5:17, KJV)

Understanding God's will is essential to our faith in God. By doing so, we will better navigate our relationship with God and others, as well as our prayer life and every area of our lives in Christ Jesus.

Believers should always remember that God does not and is not obligated to do what is contrary to His will. That being said, wouldn't understanding God's will be essential to our faith in God? If our faith in God is relational, it will be.

Paul, in the above scripture, is, in essence, telling us not to be fools. Another way to put it is to say, "Don't live like fools." That's the way those in the world live. The world lives unwisely because they do not know or understand the will of God, even His natural will, which they reject. This is why it is so important for each believer to understand what the will of God is.

To understand God's will, one must come into the knowledge of what God's will is. There are three main ways that we can know that:

1. Through nature. Those things that are seen naturally

occurring. That which is done without interference or the interjection of man's will.

2. *Nature always reflects God's divine order.* In nature, when things move out of that divine order, nature itself seeks to bring them back into order, or nature will isolate or eliminate them. God uses divine law to govern every aspect of creation, and it is those laws that maintain nature's order. Nature purges itself of disorder because disorder is in conflict with divine law. If we look, we can see that principle operating in our lives. Mankind is also a part of nature. If sought, we can clearly see God revealing Himself and His will in and throughout nature.

3. *Through God's Word.* God's will, as revealed in nature, is a general expression of His will. His will is also revealed in greater specificity through His written and spoken word. This is why it's so important to come into the knowledge and understanding of His Word. That can only take place by taking the time to do so, which requires interest. God's Word is a reflection of His revealed will. When we walk in His Word, we are walking in and in accord with His revealed and perfect will.

4. *By His Spirit.* God reveals His will to us through divine revelation and knowledge, through and by the Holy Spirit. The Holy Spirit performs specific tasks in the earth, as well as in and through the lives of believers. When believers yield themselves to the Holy Spirit, they yield themselves to the will, plan, and purpose of God.

God's Spirit constantly operates in the earth to facilitate man's understanding of God's will, be it through nature, His Word, or the inspiration of His Holy Spirit.

It is also important to know that God has a revealed will and a concealed will. God's revealed will is the will of God that is given to us to know and understand. God's revealed will is what Paul was referring to in Ephesians 5:17 (KJV) when he said, "*...be ye not unwise, but understanding what the will of the Lord is.*"

It is given to everyone to know God's revealed will. It doesn't matter if a person is religious or non-religious, a good person or bad, rich or poor, etc. Everyone can know God's revealed will.

God reveals His revealed will to use through a variety of means and can be known and discovered through life's routines, nature, reading and study of His written Word, divine revelations that are given through His spirit, dreams, words spoken by others, or any other means God chooses to use. Mankind can and should know and understand God's revealed will.

When it comes to God's concealed will, however, not everyone will be given to know it until such time He reveals it. There are also times when God may reveal a portion of His concealed will to one that He may not reveal to another. Timing may also be involved in the revealing of God's concealed will. There's one main thing we must know about God's concealed will; it is concealed. Everyone is not given to know or understand it.

Most people want to know God's will based on their own interests, not God's. Just know that God is God, and He does not have to march to our drumbeat. We march to His beat, not He to ours. This is also why it is so important for us to have faith in God and to submit to His will. In fact, we cannot know everything, but God can and does. That is also why we must trust Him.

This is a little aside, but if you don't believe that God exists, you put yourself at a disadvantage, and you have to have rejected the evidence around you that He does. It's like seeing rat droppings, but you have never seen a rat, then concluding that there is no such thing as a rat because *you* have never seen a rat. You don't have to see the rat to know that the rat exists, nor must the rat reveal itself to answer the question of its existence. The same holds true for God. Natural logic, through deductive reasoning, provides the answer. Some, however, rather use the circular logic of a nonexistent god to reject any evidence of God, though it's all around them.

- *Deductive reasoning/logic*: The process by which the premise is validated or invalidated through logical deduction to reach a conclusion, allowing the evidence to bring one to the conclusion. Reaching an objective conclusion.
- *Circular reasoning/logic:* The process by which the premise is perceived as true, and therefore, anything to the contrary is rejected, or no independent grounds or evidence is used to reach the conclusion. Reaching a subjective conclusion.

We should resolve our mind's dilemmas the same way we solve any other problem: through deductive reasoning/logic, not circular reasoning/logic. We deduce from the evidence that we have or is given to reach our conclusions. If we don't know the rat because we have never seen a rat, then cast aside the evidence of the rat's existence because we don't believe the rat exists, how then would we know the rat, even if we see the rat? The likelihood is that we will reject the rat because there is no evidence that the rat is the rat. It is the same way with God. People reject God because they do not want to accept Him. To accept God would mean that they are accountable. That's the real issue. It's easy to reject God's will when one rejects God's existence. They don't have to answer or submit to a nonexistent God.

The challenge for most people is not knowing God's will but submitting to God's will. When most people ask about God's will, they do so for selfish reasons; they want to know something about their future: what will happen or what they should do, etc. In such cases, they should ask, "What will I *do* if I do know?" Understand this, if one doesn't obey God's written Word, why would they heed His spoken word?

God's will is that which establishes His Word, and His Word is an expression and reflection of his revealed will. If a person has little to no interest in reading God's Word, then they will also have little to no interest in hearing His voice. So, to understand God's will, one must at least understand His Word; doing so will tune one into God's Holy Spirit, and in the process, they will gain a better and a greater understanding of His will.

The Lesson of Gethsemane 1

When Jesus was praying in Gethsemane, He understood God's will. His prayers weren't to change God's will but to enquire if there was a way to do God's will without drinking the bitter cup He was about to drink. Our approach should be the same. To understand this, you must understand the oneness Jesus had with the Father.

What I'm about to say about oneness may sound a bit contradictory, but only due to the way we see things in the natural. In the natural, we see things in two to three dimensions. The spirit does not have such limitations. In the world of the spirit, there is the ability to see things transcendently, beyond the dimensional limits to which we are accustomed in the natural world.

Oneness doesn't mean the loss of individuality of thought, will, or desire, but rather a symphony of such. In fact, a good way to illustrate oneness is a musical instrument. A piano has eighty-five keys or more. Each of those keys has an individual tone, feel, etc. If, while one plays, each key does its own thing in its own way, the melody will be lost, and there will be sound but no music. But through the hand of the musician, the cacophonous sounds of individuality are transformed into a beautiful harmony. Those singular discordant sounds merged to create beautiful music by the musician.

If each note in a musical score were alive, each would have to surrender and turn over its will to the musician while retaining its ability to act, but only as the musician dictates. The musician then activates the ability of each key as the musician determines, negating any need for further submission from the keys. The musician then utilizes the abilities of the keys, creating the desired melody.

Just as discordant sounds are melded together at the hand of a skilled musician to create beautiful music through oneness, God establishes His will, plan, and purpose through those that believe in Him. That is a part of what happened in Gethsemane, and that is what must take place in each of our lives.

Jesus' prayer in Gethsemane wasn't an effort to exercise will, then later subordinate it, but rather explore another possibility of accomplishing the Father's objective. That fact is made more clearly in Mark 14:35–36. Jesus knew that there was nothing impossible; His request in prayer was to ask about the possibility, not to exercise His will or to change the will of the Father.

The Lesson of Gethsemane 2 (Remaining in Submission to the Father)

One day, John the Baptist looked out and, seeing Jesus, he turned to a delegation of priests and Levites that were sent from Jerusalem to interview him (directing their attention to Jesus) and said, "*Behold the Lamb of God, which taketh away the sin of the world*" (John 1:29, KJV).

In Gethsemane, we see the Lamb preparing Himself and being prepared for the slaughter. Jesus indeed was the Lamb; Gethsemane was the place of preparation, and the cross was the altar. Gethsemane was also the place where Jesus taught us one of His most important and valuable lessons: How to remain in submission to the Father's will. I believe one of the most important lessons we can learn concerning things that can impact our faith in God is the submission of our will to God's will. The submission of our will to God's will is our first step to becoming one with the Father.

At its core, sin is a result of man's refusal to submit his will to God's. There is, however, a way to deal with and even avoid such a clash of wills; it is accomplished through oneness. It is impossible to have oneness and division at the same time. Jesus was never at variance with His Father because they were always at one with one another. Another byproduct of Jesus' oneness with the Father was an absolute trust, resulting in absolute submission and faith in God.

Becoming one with the Father should be the goal of every believer. I'm not talking about the "waiting until we get to heaven" type of oneness, but rather the oneness that is a result of a total and absolute submission of our will to God's will. In fact, our oneness is what Jesus prayed for while He was on *earth* (*see John 17:20–23*). Jesus first prayed for His disciples, and after doing so, He prayed for those that would believe in Him through the words proclaimed by His disciples. Let's take a brief moment to look at portions of those scripture verses:

"Neither pray I for these alone, but for them also which shall believe on me through their word." John 17:20 (KJV)

"That they all may be one; as thou, Father, art in me, and I in thee, that they also may be one in us: that the world may believe that thou hast sent me." John 17:21 (KJV)

"And the glory which thou gavest me I have given them; that they may be one, even as we are one." John 17:22 (KJV)

"I in them, and thou in me, that they may be made perfect in one; and that the world may know that thou hast sent me, and hast loved them, as thou hast loved me." John 17:23 (KJV)

Throughout this book, I have and will continue to use the word "believer." What indeed is a believer? In these few verses of scripture, Jesus outlines exactly what a believer is.

"To believe" in the previous verses is translated from the Greek word *pisteuo* (pist-yoo'-o), meaning "to have faith in, entrust (especially one's spiritual well-being to Christ), to commit (to trust), put in trust with."

Jesus here prays for the believers, those who have faith in God, who trust in Him through hearing the *logos* (log'-os), the preaching, spoken words of His disciples. Those words were captured and placed in writing for us to receive, embrace, and share with others. Think about it; if you believe in Jesus, you do so as a result of the preaching of His disciples. That means Jesus prayed for you. What an awesome thing; over 2000 years ago, Jesus prayed for you.

Next. Out of all of the things that Jesus could have prayed on behalf of those that believe, He prayed that "*...they may be one...*" Those words were some of Jesus' last words. A person's last words are some of their most important words. With all of the things that Jesus could have prayed on our behalf, He prayed that we would become one.

Becoming one with God is key to our submission to Him and sets us on a path to the application of our faith in God. If we are in oneness with God, we will be *focused* not on what we want but on what He wants. When we are in total submission to God, we will always be appropriately *aggressive*. Our godly aggressiveness will aid us in powering through the challenges that seek to come between us and our execution of God's will.

Our godly aggression will never be condescending or arrogant, but we will reflect our confidence in God and in who we are in Him. It will also help us to fight the good fight of faith, enabling us to do and accomplish His perfect and divine will. True faith is an acceptance of God's will. When we are one with Him, His will becomes our will, and we conform our will to His. Our aggressiveness, therefore, is His aggressiveness, appropriately applied to the situations or circumstances we face.

The submission of our will to God's will is not blind obedience but an act of oneness and *intelligence*. Why *intelligence*? Through His Word, we know His nature, His ways, and His character. Our knowledge of God helps us to develop the depth of relationship with Him that will develop unwavering trust in Him. That trust is not blind but rooted in clear awareness of what He has, can, and will do.

When we submit our will to God's will, we should do so *tenaciously*. Simply put, we don't give up. We don't give in. We don't give out. We hang in there until we totally and completely do and accomplish *His* will, not our will. In fact, throughout all we do, we remain *humble*. We do not elevate our will, hopes, or desires above His. We humble ourselves under the mighty hands of God. That is truly what faith is all about. Every believer must be *"Focused," "Aggressive," "Intelligent," "Tenacious," and "Humble."* That is truly having faith in God and is truly *Faith Made Easy*.

CHAPTER 24:

FROM SUBMISSION TO ONENESS

Oneness in the context of this book is the merging of the believer's will, plans, purpose, and desires with God's. It is a sameness that produces a singleness with God and the believer. Oneness is different than unity and being unified. They may seem the same, but they are vastly different.

Unity is different from oneness in that unity lacks the merging necessary to form the singularity that produces oneness. Unity brings together without merging into true oneness. Unity also requires a consistent commonality that produces the cohesiveness necessary to establish unity.

The word "unity" is mentioned only three times in the Scripture (when using the KJV). It's used once in the Old Testament in Psalm 133:1 as used in today's context. In each of the other two, Ephesians 4:3, 13, the word "unity" translates into the word "oneness."

Oneness can be difficult to grasp. In mathematics, using any number other than one will produce a multiple of itself: 2×2=4, 4×2=8, etc. In each case, the numbers are manipulated to form another number. But if the number one is used, the process is the same, but the outcome will be very different:1×2=2, 4×1=4, etc.

As you can see, the number one produces sameness. That sameness is what Christ was referring to when He prayed for us in John 17. If we are one with Jesus, we will equal Jesus. If Jesus is one with the Father, Jesus will equal the Father; as a result, we all will be one. That oneness is what our heavenly Father is seeking to achieve. Unity cannot achieve such a result because the individual nature and ability of the number remain, making it vulnerable to division and conversion into something else. That cannot happen with oneness.

So, as believers become one with Jesus Christ, they cannot be or become what He is not. As a result of their oneness with Christ, believers will enter into oneness with each other. As they enter into oneness with Christ, they will also enter into oneness with the Father because Christ and the Father are one. That is what 1 John 5:7–8 is referring to.

As believers, when we become one with the Father, we will see what He sees; we will want what He wants, do what He does, etc. When in oneness, the Father's will, will become the believer's will.

In the case of the believer's relationship with God, oneness is not just the total submission to, agreement with, and acceptance of God's will, hopes, and desires; it is the merging of God's will, hope, and desires into and as their own. Any aspect of their will that conflicts with God's will should be jettisoned. Oneness cannot take place otherwise. That is a choice that every believer must make: to choose God's will or their own.

Submission subordinates; unity brings together; oneness merges and melds to form a singular whole new thing (as it relates to the believer, Christ). In actuality, the process of becoming one begins with the submission that produces a unity that evolves into oneness. Until believers enter into the state of oneness, they are vulnerable to losing unity, which would cause the loss of submission, which would result in a new separation.

I said earlier that when believers submit to God, they do not elevate their will or their hopes or desires above God's; instead, they humble themselves under His mighty hands. That is also what faith in God is all about. There is, however, an easier, better approach to our faith in God. What is it? It is entering into and being in true oneness with God. Submission to God's will is just a start. Those that believe in God must strive to become one with God.

Think about this: Jesus was one with the Father; He said so in John 17. When reading the Scriptures, we never read where Jesus stated that He submitted Himself to the Father. Why? Because He and His Father were and are One. Why is this so important? Because submission is only necessary when a person under authority wants to do something contrary to what the person in authority wants. When the person under authority wants the same thing as the person in authority, submission is unnecessary because they are at one, at least in that issue. In addition to John 17, consider the following verse: John 5:30 (KJV), *"I can of mine own self do nothing: as I hear, I judge: and my judgment is just; because I seek not mine own will, but the will of the Father which hath sent me."*

Because they are at one, there is a sameness of will, hope, and desire, resulting in oneness. While in oneness, there is no real need for submission. That is the relationship Jesus had with the Father, and that is the relationship every believer must have with one another. It is necessary so that we can enter into the relationship Jesus has with His Father.

True oneness with God is reached when the believer's will, hopes, and desires not only reflect the will, hope, and desire of their heavenly Father but are their heavenly Father's will, hope, and desire.

Oneness should be the goal of every believer. If believers cannot become one with each other, it will greatly affect their ability to accomplish God's will in their lives and the earth. It will also make it near impossible to enter into God's desired level of oneness that Jesus prayed that we would have. Somehow, we will get there because Jesus' prayer for our oneness will be answered.

Once we as believers become one with each other, we can then enter the oneness that Jesus had with the Father. In fact, the believer's oneness will be accomplished through first submitting their will to God's will and walking in obedience to His Word. From there, there should be a total and complete embracing and merging into God's will. It is then and only then that we can even hope to enter into true oneness with God.

But there's another reason believers must become one: so that the world may believe. In John 17:21 and 23, Jesus said, "*...that the world may believe that thou hast sent me*" (verse 21, KJV). "*...and that the world may know that thou hast sent me, and hast loved them, as thou hast loved me*" (verse 23, KJV). The world's ability to believe in Jesus depends upon the oneness of believers. The ability for the world to see God's love for Christ, us, and them will also depend greatly upon the oneness of believers.

Oneness to believers is not just a good thing; it is a must if they are to be effective ministers in this world. The world walks by sight. For the world, seeing is believing. If the world does not see Christ in and through believers, how then will they ever see Christ? Believers are the world's Christ in the earth; we must let the world see Him. Oneness in Christ is not advisory; it is a must, and it's key to believers having faith in God.

Action Plan 13:
God Does the Work; We Get the Spotlight

"For it is God which worketh in you both
"to will and to do of his good pleasure."
Philippians 2:13 (KJV)

Once we begin to truly have faith in God, we will begin to see significant victories in our lives. During such times of success, it is easy for us to think that we are the ones accomplishing the things that are being done. It is important to not fall into that trap of the enemy. We do what we do through Him, the Lord who is the strength of our lives. It is He that enables us to live a life that is pleasing to God. We must work diligently to stay in oneness with God, especially when things are not going so well. We should also do the following:

1. *Set a goal of seeing the perfect will, plan, and purpose of God reflected in everything that we do.* Doing so prevents us from placing our will over God's will.

2. *Be committed to living a life of obedience to God.* Measure everything we think, say, and do by God's Word. Let our conclusions be in perfect alignment with God's Word. Obedience is necessary when we have the ability and will to do otherwise. Remember our obedience to God reflects our love for Him.

3. *Submit our will to God's will.* Submission is necessary when we are under the authority of another. In this case, to submit is to subordinate our will, hopes, wants, and desires to the Lord's. It is placing all that we are and have under His will and authority.

4. *Seek to enter into oneness with God.* To do so, we adopt God's will as our will. Doing this one thing will revolutionize our walk of faith and give us confidence that will be difficult to imagine. Doing numbers one to three will get us on the road to doing so.

5. *Learn to change the dynamics of the things that we face through giving thanks to God even if we brought the situation upon ourselves.* Giving thanks moves us from defense to offense. Giving God thanks will change our approach to dealing with the results. Doing so also shifts the resolution of the situation from us to the Lord.

6. *Note: This doesn't mean that we can do things with the intention of God getting us out of a pickle.* That's deceit, and we will be the ones deceived, and it will not work. Remember God looks at our heart.

7. *Learn to not waver.* That takes discipline, but we can do it. To not waver, we must choose not to doubt, choose to believe. Look through and beyond our situation to see and embrace God's limitless ability and willingness to do on our behalf whatever truly needs to be done.

8. *Trust God.* None of this will make a difference if we do not trust Him. Do so regardless of the outcome.

Chapter 24: From Submission to Oneness

"Nevertheless when the
"Son of man cometh, shall he
"find faith on the earth?"
Luke 18:8 (KJV)

CHAPTER 25:

THE PERSONIFICATION OF FAITH

There was a time in the church, and probably still is, when one would be asked to define faith, and the answer would quickly be given, *"...faith is the substance of things hoped for, the evidence of things not seen,"* quoting portions of Hebrews 11:1 (KJV).

Then there were doctrines crafted around the *"Now Faith"* portion of the same verse. The problem with both responses to the verse is that the verse is not a definition at all, nor does it relate to one's self-confidence or confident belief that what they are believing for will take place. Hebrews 11:1 does not refer to the level of a believer's confidence that anything will or will not take place. The *"Now"* portion of the scripture does not refer to timing; rather, it expresses a contrast between the earlier verses and the present one. It also directs attention or emphasizes the believer's relational faith, commitment, and conviction towards God.

Hebrews 11:1 relates to what was being said in chapter 10 and refers to the believer's trust in God and the hope of the gospel, not in one's level of confidence. Hebrews 11, which believers call the faith chapter, refers to having faith in God.

Everyone in what some call "the hall of fame of faith" is there as a result of their faith in God, not confident belief in their own ability to make something happen or not happen, for that matter. True faith in God is not a work of the head but the soul. It is a mark of one's trust in God, not in one's self.

So what is faith? At its root, true faith is confidence in God. Some believe, however, that faith is the opposite of fear. Is faith simply the opposite of fear? Fear is an emotion; is faith also an emotion? Of course not. If faith is, as it is said to be, substance and evidence, it cannot then be an emotion. Additionally, if faith is an emotion, it would be unstable because it would vary based upon the circumstances.

If faith then is not an emotion, it can't be the opposite of fear. Faith must then be something totally different than fear, not just its opposite. Is then faith one's confidence that they will get whatever they're seeking? If so, then all such confidence must be faith. If, however, that is not the case (and it isn't), then faith is not merely one's confidence or one's own ability not to doubt. How then would it differ from positive thinking?

The reason believers have so much difficulty with faith is that they confuse what should be faith in God with their level of self-confidence. They often make matters worse when they compare their individual level of confidence to their perception of the level of confidence of others. They then conclude that the reason they did not get what they wanted was due to their inability to believe that what they wanted would happen or that God would do what they wanted to be done. They resolve in their heart that if they could have doubted less and employed more confidence, they would have gotten what they asked for.

My friend, employing increasing amounts of confidence, self-confidence, or otherwise is not the same as having faith in God. It may be presumption and even foolishness, but it is not faith in God. Such an approach will undermine one's faith in God. Why? Because at its core, it directs confidence to self or others rather than directing it solely to believe what God said. I often say, "If you could do it and wanted it to be done, it wouldn't have to be done because it would already be done. It would be done because you would do it or have it done. Confidence alone is not true faith, and it is certainly not faith in God."

Many times God does not give us what we want because it is not in accord with His will for our life, the lives of others, or His will in the earth. Remember 1 John 5:14 (KJV), "*And this is the confidence that we have in him, that, if we ask anything according to his will, he heareth us*." Should God subordinate His will for our will? Should He ignore His Word and give us what is not in His will because we have a perceived need or ask Him to? Should God limit His ability to help us to *our* notions of what His help should be? I say not, even though I must admit I at times want Him to.

I once had several family-related medical financial issues converging upon me at the same time, and I could not put them off due to their critical nature. When I calculated all of the funds from all of my accounts, I was woefully short of the funds necessary and had to leave shortly for one of the first appointments and had to pay cash for the treatments when I got to the doctor's office.

Each of the members of my family was depending on me, and I had already exceeded my limit and was not even out of the gate. I could pay for the first treatment, but then what? I paused a moment to consider if I should discuss the issue with my wife but concluded that I would not because I did not want her to worry. I thought and thought, and then I prayed, "Lord, they depend on me; I will depend on You." Then I got up to leave for the appointment.

When we arrived at the doctor's office, we were called into an office to discuss the charges and to pay before the procedure could begin. It was then that we were told how much the procedure would be; the price was doubled what was previously given. After some discussion about the price difference and further discussing the price with the one that gave the first price, all to no avail, I, in perfect peace, wrote a check for the requested amount. By the time I finished writing the check, we were told that we would be given a 30 percent discount because we were paying cash. That was indeed a blessing. I thought again, *Lord, they depend on me; I will depend on You.*

Shortly after writing the check, the door to the office opened again; it was the person that gave the original price. The issue had been discussed with the physician, who decided to do each procedure at what would be a discount of approximately 70 percent. What a blessing. I voided that check and wrote another one for a fraction of the first. Then we were off to another room for the procedure.

After the procedure was completed, the doctor was discussing the process that would be taking place in the future and assured us that they would do their best to keep our out-of-pocket expenses as low as possible. He then asked if we could wait a few moments so that they could check some other rate structures, and they would base the charges on their lowest rate. Their attendant returned with a new price that was a fraction of what the previously lowered price was. We would now be able to have all of the procedures performed for less than the cost of one procedure. What a great blessing. I again thought to myself, *Lord, they depend on me; I will depend on You.* The Lord indeed showed Himself strong in our lives that day.

Some would ask, why didn't the Lord simply perform a divine healing? Good question. If He did, however, would I be able to give you this testimony? There may be those that will read or hear this testimony that will believe the Lord to reduce their bill but not to divinely heal.

At the time of this writing, we are in the beginning stages of the challenge. My expectation is for healing divinely or otherwise. Healing is healing; I will share with the Lord my will and desire but leave it up to the Lord to determine the method He uses to manifest it. I will also trust unwaveringly in Him during the process.

We may want many things, but do we really know what we're asking for? Many times, we don't because we haven't considered the ramifications of what we are asking for. That's why we must trust God totally and completely. He knows what we do not. He also knows how best to deliver. That's what faith in God is all about. Faith in God places God above all. That's why we trust Him. That is what faith in God is all about. Faith in God places God's will above our will. It is so important to apply Proverbs 3:5–7 by asking the Lord for His direction and understanding in everything.

God's promise to us in *1 Corinthians 10:13* is to not permit us to be tested, enticed, etc., more than we can bear. If giving us what we ask results in that which is more than could be borne, should He do so anyway? Not only will I say that He should not, but He will not and cannot violate His Word to satisfy our wants. The question for us then is whether or not we are willing to trust Him enough to be willing to accept His will.

In the final analysis, true faith is firm, complete acceptance of, and agreement with the will of God. It is trusting God that He knows what He is doing. It is also the acceptance of and agreement with God that He is, that He can, and that He will do what He said He would do. That is true faith in God.

Testimony (Update)

Several weeks after the medical procedure I shared with you earlier, we returned as scheduled to the medical facility for the next procedure. Before the procedure began, additional tests were conducted. After a series of tests, we were escorted to another room to wait before the procedure was to begin.

Not long afterward, the doctor came in and stated (*in essence*) that he no longer thought the additional procedures, at least at that time, would be needed. He then told us to come back for a follow-up in six months… What a blessing! "Lord, they depend on me; I depend on You."

There isn't always a straight line to our outcomes when we stand in faith. That's why we must always trust God. God knows how to deliver the godly out of adversity (2 Peter 2:9). That's why we must trust God. That is also why we must have and keep our faith in God.

Faith in God and Saving Faith

If I told you that you must have the confidence within yourself to get yourself saved or make your salvation happen, you would quickly inform me that I was in error. However, we do just that in our traditional approach to faith. We believe that we need to have the confidence within ourselves to get what we are hoping for or to make it happen.

With salvation, it is not our faith that saves us, but rather our belief and acceptance of what God has done and said concerning salvation. What I'm saying is, just as we believe in our hearts that God has saved us, we must also believe in our hearts that God will do what He said about supplying our needs and empowering us to do and achieve what we seek in accordance to His will. It is the same faith.

The same belief that we employ when believing God for salvation is the same belief that we must employ for everything else. It all comes down to our faith in God. The main and possibly only difference is that God imparts saving faith to us through the preaching of the gospel. It is that saving faith that is the seed of faith that will grow within us as our relationship with God grows.

It all comes down to who and what we believe. Believe God or the devil. Believe God or believe the circumstances. The choice and the decision are ours. We each must make that choice. When we do, it will be reflected in our lives. Each of us must develop a personal, intimate relationship with God to truly have faith in God.

> *"Now faith is the substance of things hoped for, the "evidence of things not seen." (Hebrews 11:1, KJV)*

CHAPTER 26:

DEFINING FAITH

If there is a proper definition that defines "faith in God," I believe it would be: (1) a firm, unwavering trust in God; (2) an unwavering belief and confidence that God can and will do what He said; (3) the acceptance and aligning of one's mind, soul, heart, and actions with God's will; (4) bringing into an agreement the natural man with the spiritual man to establish God's will.

At its core, faith in God is entering into oneness with God. One simply cannot have faith in God while disagreeing or doubting God. When having faith in God, one will never doubt that God is, that He can, or that God will do what He is determined to do. If, in any instance, you have unwavering certainty that God is, that God can, and that God will do what He said that He would do and you are doing so in obedience or submission to Him, you can rest assured that you have faith in God.

As you may have seen in Hebrews 11:1, two things are always prevalent when faith is present: substance and evidence.

When believing for anything, if there isn't both substance and evidence for what you are hoping for, faith cannot be present; in such a case, you are merely wishing for what you are hoping for. There will always be substance and evidence for what you are hoping for when faith is present. Faith is both the substance and the evidence for what you are hoping for. It is safe to conclude, therefore, that if there is no substance or evidence, there is no faith.

"Substance" is "the real, tangible, actual constitution (point of creation)" of the thing being hoped for. It is the solid basis for the certainty of the thing being hoped for. The Greek word for substance, as used in Hebrews 11:1, is *hupostasis (hoop-os'-tas-is): a setting under (support), concretely, essence, or abstractly, assurance, confidence, confident person* (Strong's Concordance).

It is your *hupostasis* (assurance and confidence) in God that serves as the basis for your belief that you will receive the thing being hoped for. Your confidence can be as solid as concrete when it is founded upon a confident belief that God can and that God will bring you into the manifestation of the thing for which you are hoping. You can see this in the life of Abraham, and it must also be present in your life if you are committed to walking in faith.

There is one thing to remember, however; this is not guessing what God said or will do; this is knowing and accepting what God has said about what He would or would not do. Always ask yourself what God said about what you are hoping for. Once that question is answered, and you embrace fully what God has said about it, you will stand as solid as a rock, and you will stand in oneness with God for the thing you are believing Him for.

Simply put, you must believe what God has done in order to believe God for what He will do. That's why our testimonies and reading the Bible are so important. How can we embrace God's Word if we don't hear or read God's Word? How can you embrace God's Word if you avoid or reject what you hear about God or read in His Word? How can you embrace God's Word if you do not value it?

God's Word is substance; often, it will be the only substance and evidence that you'll have when facing your challenges or when seeking to do what seems impossible or unlikely. God's Word and embracing what God has done in the past will often be the only things that you will have when walking in faith. That's also why faith is relational. While developing a relationship with God, you will also develop a relationship with His Word; the two are inseparable. So true faith will always have substance.

Faith is also evidentiary. The word "evidence" is from *Middle English,* and it means "obvious to the eye or mind." It is also defined as "the available body of facts or information indicating whether a belief or proposition is true or valid."

The Greek word for "evidence," as used in Hebrews 11:1, is *elegchos (el'-eng-khos),* meaning *proof, conviction, reproof* (Strong's Concordance). Evidence then is an indicator of material facts that are unseen to the natural eye. So if those facts are not seen, then what are they? Well, if your faith is in God, then the evidence is what God has consistently done in the past; therefore, it is reasonable to conclude that God will do the same thing again. If a believer or anyone else cannot reach that conclusion, they are not in faith and cannot have faith in God. That is why Jesus told His disciples in Mark 11:22 (KJV) to "*Have faith in God.*"

If you can truly accept what God has done, you can believe God for what must be done. That's what faith in God is all about. Many times, if not most, the only evidence you will have for your conviction is what God has done. The task then becomes to not produce a reason for Him to not do it again.

The evidence of faith will help to keep you from migrating from hope into hopelessness. However, if you are in a place of hopelessness, the evidence of faith will also lift you out of hopelessness into a place of hope.

You can also know that faith is in operation when there is the presence of substance that relates to the thing for which you are hoping. It may be spiritual substance, but it is substance nonetheless. Because that type of substance is not seen, faith will also provide the evidence, enabling you to believe or continue to believe. Remember, however, because that substance is spiritual, its evidence will also be spiritual.

To initiate faith in God, you must see and believe what God has done, then conclude that He can and will do it again. More importantly, resolve that He will do it for you and do so in your situations. When you do, you can be assured that you are having and walking in your faith in God.

CHAPTER 27:

HIDING THE WORD (DON'T FORGET TO REMEMBER)

"Thy word have I hid in mine heart, that I might not sin against thee" (Psalm 119:11, KJV).

"And the cares of this world, and the deceitfulness of riches, and the lusts of other things entering in, choke the word, and it becometh unfruitful" (Mark 4:19, KJV).

"For this people's heart is waxed gross, and their ears are dull of hearing, and their eyes they have closed; lest at any time they should see with their eyes, and hear with their ears, and should understand with their heart, and should be converted, and I should heal them" (Matthew 13:15, KJV).

Memory and how we utilize our memory are invaluable to our faith in God. It is important that we remember, but *what* we remember is also important. Memory is an act of retrieving what has already been retained. Three things that must be remembered by those that are living and walking by faith: (1) they must remember God's Word; (2) they must remember what God has said; (3) they must remember to reject the things that are contrary to one and two. As said in Psalm 119:1, we must hide His word in our hearts so that we will not sin against Him. Doing so will also help us grow in faith.

I realize that to some, much of what I have shared thus far is a bit different than what we're accustomed to hearing about faith. What I'm about to tell you now will not be an exception; it is important, however, that I do in order that we understand better the process of developing faith. Once we get a clear picture of this, it will make it easier to live by faith as believers. I believe that there is a process to living by faith and seeing the things that we hope for become a reality.

It is generally accepted in Christianity that man is a triune being. That's a fancy way of saying that man is a single individual comprised of three distinct parts. Those parts should and usually do work so seamlessly together that they are viewed as a single person. To most, the physical body is considered to be that person.

You may have heard it said that man is a spirit that has a soul and lives in a body. I have a slightly different take on that. I say that man is a soul who has a mind that possesses a body. For there to be faith in God, the mind and soul must move into and remain in agreement with each other. The physical body pretty much follows suit with what the other two do. So how does this take place, and how does such an agreement work to produce faith in our lives?

The cross section of the image above is an illustration of the relation of the soul, mind, and body. It also illustrates the relationship of the heart as the repository of the soul.

My hypothesis is that man is a soul, and within him is a repository that I am referring to as the heart. The triune nature of man is a perfect example of the oneness discussed throughout this book. The physical, mental, and soulical (a word I coined years ago to express that which relates to the soul) portions work seamlessly together to the point that when one looks at the physical, they see all three parts of him. This is indeed a reflection of what God was saying in Genesis 1:26 (KJV), *"Let us make man in our image, and after our likeness..."*

The heart, I believe, is not separate from the soul but is a part of the soul, somewhat like the brain is to the physical body. It is in the heart that the soul stores information to be used as a basis upon which decisions are made. It is also in the heart that man communes with God and that God enters into communion with man and sets up His abode.

The heart is the place where man stores God's word, be it spoken, written, or inspired. It is primarily through the heart the Holy Spirit enters into a man and abides. As an aside, I do understand both the oneness and the difference between God and the Holy Spirit, but I will not get into it here.

It is important to note here, however, that to complete man, the soul would need a physical body by which he could navigate the physical realm. He would also need a mind to serve as a link between him and his physical body. Lastly, both the physical body and the mind must have the ability to gather, retain, and understand information and knowledge. That ability to retain and remember God's Word is key to our faith in God. That's why it's so important to hide God's Word in our hearts, as reflected in Psalm 119:11.

The word "hid" in Psalm 119:11, in Hebrew, is *tsaphan* (tsaw-fan'), to hide (by covering over), to hoard or reserve, figuratively to deny, specifically (favorably) to protect, (unfavorably) to lurk, esteem, hide(-den one, self), lay up, lurk, (be set) privily, (keep) secret(-ly, place) (Strong's Concordance).

As we consider this definition, we can see what the Holy Spirit, through the psalmist, is saying, "First, it is important to understand that to hide does mean to cover, to place secretly or conceal, but it is done in the sense of protection from loss and to deny anything access that may diminish its value."

Jesus illustrated the importance of this in His Parable of the Sower. In the parable, the seed (word) that *"fell by the wayside"* (outside of an understanding heart) "*the fowls of the air came and devoured it up*" (KJV). It is vitally important to "hide" God's Word in your heart; that means that you must understand God's Word and embrace it, not reject it.

"To hide" in Psalm 119:11 also means "to keep, lay up, reserve, or place in-store." It is what we must do if there is to be any hope of living a truly victorious life and do so in a way that is pleasing to God.

Psalm 119:11 also tells us what we are to store and where we are to store it. The what is God's Word. The where is our heart. The psalmist also states who has the responsibility of doing the storing. That responsibility falls upon the person who has the heart where the Word is to be stored. You cannot bring God's Word to memory if it is not stored. This is not the memorization of God's Word; it is the collection and accumulation of God's Word in the heart. It is like placing God in your vault, which is different than remembering that God exists. It is not enough to memorize Scripture; Scripture must become a part of your life. That can only be done by making a conscious effort to allow God's Word into your heart and integrating it into every part of your being.

Lastly, as reflected in Matthew 13:15, when we don't "hide" God's Word in our hearts, we will increasingly harden, and that that God wants to do in our lives will not be realized because there will be no word to draw from to affect the change that needs to take place in our life. You can't bring it to memory when it was never placed in your heart or if it was stolen out of your heart.

It is important to hide God's Word in your heart, remember it is there, and use it to accomplish God's will for your life and to accomplish His will in the earth.

Thought to Remember

Focusing on the circumstances will result in the acceptance of the circumstances. Accepting the circumstances will result in the replacement of what God said with the circumstances. That will result in unbelief and loss of faith.

CHAPTER 28:

THE TRIUNITY OF MAN

The image at the end of this section is an illustrative dissection of my perception of mankind that illustrates what I call the triunity (three parts) of man. As previously stated, man is a triune being, meaning that he is a soul that has a mind and possesses a body. Those three are one. They do not just operate as one; they are one.

The soul is man's seat of consciousness (awareness, objective and subjective thought, understanding, feeling, desire, affection, and aversion). Man's mind is also his arbiter (capacity and faculty of rational thought [inherent ability], understanding, feeling of desire, animus, and thinking). It can be said that man's mind is a type of imprimatur (certifier of what is or is not acceptable based on the standards set by the soul).

Man's physical body is his seat of natural cognition, housing his physical ability to sense, feel, desire, think objectively and subjectively, understand, express affection, aversion, etc. Those three areas working together enable man to function in accord with God and in the image and likeness of God on both the natural and spiritual planes.

This is an aside, but it's important to note that the nature and character of the soul (image and likeness) are reflected and expressed indivisibly and collectively in each: the mind and physical body of man. That's necessary for there to be seamless communication and oneness between every aspect of man within himself and, by extension, His God.

The mind takes on and embodies the nature and qualities of the soul while the physical body reflects and expresses the same in the natural realm while linking the soul to it. Things move from spiritual to natural, God to our soul, the soul to the mind, the mind to the body, the body to the world. Those that are in Christ are indeed the lights of this world.

The flow of information depicted below shows that the physical body receives sensory information through its five senses. That information is either transferred to or gathered by the mind then vetted. The gathered information is weighed against a predetermined standard (set by the soul) of right and wrong and is rejected or embraced. If the information is embraced by the soul, confirmation is relayed back to the mind, which sends a response back to the physical body, which responds accordingly.

The information flow of the illustration seems to indicate that the information flow of man begins externally; however, the opposite is true. Man's information flow begins internally with the soul because man's consciousness lies within the soul. Everything the mind and body do or do not do is a result of an action or inaction of the soul. It is the soul that sets the standards for what is right or wrong, good or bad, etc. Those standards are then used by the mind and physical body to assist in what they accept or reject. Information, instructions, etc., are sent from the soul to the mind, which interfaces with the body to perform the biddings of the soul. Information can also flow from the body to the mind to the soul. Again, it is the soul that determines what information is accepted, rejected, or applied.

The following illustration also shows a round, circular shape in each section, representing areas of information storage and retention (memory) at each portion of man's being.

DISSECTION OF MAN:

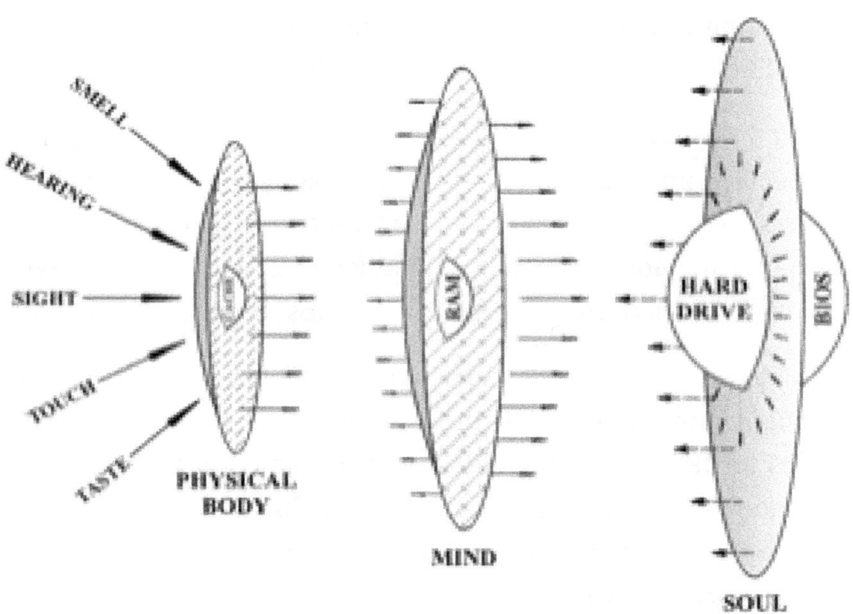

The Triunity Of Man (Information Flow)

The Memory of the Body

What I am about to share now may seem a bit weird and somewhat off the deep end, but it may help you to better understand the human deliberative process. I'll be comparing how computers store information to how the human body stores information. I believe that how we store information on both the natural and spiritual levels can be key to our faith in God and to our walking in faith.

What I'll share is extra-biblical and a bit techy, but it should be straightforward and easy to follow. The goal is to illustrate how our bodies store information by showing how computers store information. My premise is that our body (the whole man, soul, mind, and flesh, not the fleshly portion alone) stores and retrieves information. Understanding this concept will assist every believer in building and solidifying their faith in God. So let's go make some faith.

At the time of this writing, there are three main areas of memory storage in computers: RAM, cache, and hard drive. *RAM*, Random Access Memory, is what some consider to be the main area of computer memory. It is normally associated with volatile types of memory, where stored information is lost if power is removed.

Then there is the computer's *cache* memory. Cache memory is usually a more limited memory storage area that is strategically placed for fast retrieval and vetting. Cache memory stores data so that future requests for data can be served faster. The data stored in a cache might be the result of an earlier computation or a duplicate of data stored elsewhere.

Lastly, there is the largest, most recognized type of memory, the *hard drive*. The hard drive is a type of non-volatile memory retaining stored data even when powered off. It is the heart and life of the computer. All of the operating systems, applications, and vital operational information are stored on the hard drive. It holds the information even if the computer loses power or if it is taken out of the computer altogether. The information stored in the hard drive is really what makes the personal computer personal. Another way of saying that is the information stored in the hard drive is what personalizes the computer, making it your personal computer.

There is one additional thing that we must understand in this computer analogy; it is a little-known sliver of programing called *BIOS*. The BIOS is where the computer's firmware and other key information are stored. The name BIOS is an acronym meaning Basic Input-Output System. It is the information that the computer needs to make the system ready to perform all of its key functions. BIOS to the computer is close to what DNA is to the physical body.

As a little aside, in the final analysis, man's physical body simply goes along for the ride as it relates to final decision-making capacity. Decisions can be made by the physical body, but they can be overridden almost without effort by the mind and soul. This is why it is so important to be careful when taking drugs and even consuming certain foods. Some things can hinder or even break down the communication links between man's physical body, mind, and soul.

Let's get back to my computer analogy. My hypothesis is that man's soul contains his hard drive (heart), his vast store of all of his experiences and his acceptance or rejection of what is true, and his sense of what is right and wrong. It is his store for God's Word, the light of his life, and his inspirations.

It is man's soul that enters into a relationship with God and believes or rejects the things of God, including His Word. It is man's soul that sets the standard that his being, his mind, and physical body will live by and determine his norms. It is his soul that truly determines whether or not he is or is not walking in faith. This is what we call the inner man. If life is to be changed, or if one will truly have faith in God, it will happen there in the soul.

The mind is man's gatekeeper to his soul; it is the location of man's RAM. The mind gathers and stores information for and from the soul to use as a standard and guide to determine what will be accepted by and entered into the soul. This is key because the things that enter the soul can and many times do change the individual and can give a false sense of direction.

The mind also has the ability to reject outright those things that are in clear conflict with the standards the soul has previously set. The mind, independent of the soul, can believe or not believe and accept or not accept, but it should do so based on its oneness with the soul.

If a person's mind and soul are out of sync (oneness), uncertainty will be created, and it will be reflected throughout their physical body in everything they do or don't do. But how does that factor into our faith in God?

First, we develop faith in God through our acceptance of and entering into agreement with what God says. However, for that agreement to take place, there must be an agreement that takes place within ourselves. Our mind and soul must be at one. That means that they must not be in conflict. If they are, the physical body will follow suit, manifesting the intents of the heart (soul), resulting in ambiguity and lack of confidence, producing doubt. However, oneness of mind and soul produces the confidence that we traditionally consider to be faith. Now, if that confidence is based on what God has truly said, it produces faith in God.

It's important to note that it is the responsibility of the soul to bring the mind into agreement with it, not the reverse. It does so by controlling the mind's emotions, feeding it the information necessary to balance its thoughts, and most importantly, exercising its will, authority, and overall ability to bring the mind into subjection. This is what we call discipline in the natural. This becomes much easier when the soul has fully submitted to God's will and is in oneness with God.

A Glimpse into the Soul
(Seat of Objective Thought)

It begins with the soul, man's seat of objective thought. I refer to the soul as the seat of man's objective thought because the soul must make judgments that are not influenced by feelings or opinions but facts. Souls that are redeemed make judgments that are based upon God's Word and are led by God.

The soul is the incorporeal, ethereal part of man (not physical). This is why the soul is referred to as breath or spirit. In the New Testament Greek, it is referred to as *psuche* (psoo-khay'), meaning "breath, i.e., spirit."

The soul is the real you. It is man's seat of choice, the generator and the place of man's emotions, intellect, deep thought, desires, affections, aversions, and awareness. It is that which gives the mind and body their consciousness and awareness. Without the soul, the other parts of the body will simply be rendered irrelevant and cease to exist.

The soul is indeed the crown jewel of every man and is what distinguishes man from animals. Never believe that mankind is just another type of animal. Such a belief is a doctrine of devils.

The Heart of the Soul

As said before, the soul is thought to be the heart of man, but in reality, the soul contains the heart of man. It is through the heart that man can best communicate with God and that God can best communicate with man. The heart of man's soul is like his hard drive, the repository of the Word and presence of God, housing man's holy of holies.

What I am about to convey to you now is very revelatory and may be extraordinarily difficult to grasp and difficult to explain, but I'll give it my best. Consider this to be the gospel according to pastor Bennett. "*The gospel according to pastor Bennett" is an expression I coined to express that what I am about to share may be a paraphrase or an extrapolation based upon Scripture, but there may or may not be a direct scriptural reference to it. There is, however, scriptural basis for it, and it adheres to true scriptural fidelity*.

Imagine there is a place within mankind that serves as a special access point for God and the things of God to be received and kept within man. Imagine that place being the repository of all of man's true and divine wisdom, knowledge, insights, inspiration, etc.

Imagine also that if such a place did exist within man, it would be a place where God could reside, making man God's temple and the place of the infilling of the Holy Spirit. It would be a place that needs to be continually cleansed by the washing of God's Word.

Such a place would also be the place that evil spirits would love to occupy and would have to be cast out if they did. This would be that place where faith is created and guarded with all diligence. It would be the place where man communicates and fellowships with God.

Now, because man is a free agent, he and he alone controls what goes in and out of that place as well as what is stored in it. Such a place would be a special and peculiar part of man's being. If such a place exists within man, that place would be the heart of every man, the place that contains that which man uses to determine all that he does.

That would be the place where man determines what he considers to be right, wrong, good, bad, etc. It would be a place so valuable and important that it should be obscure, guarded, and protected. There is such a place within every man's soul that was once reserved especially for the presence of God. It is also the primary place through which God speaks to man.

Prior to man's fall, that place would have been filled with God's presence. But due to his own aims and desires, man, through his disobedience, rejected God. After man's fall, or rather his rejection of God, man began to fill that place with his own will, wants, and desires.

We really shouldn't have to imagine such a place; it can be found in each of us. This place is a part of man's soul, and it is why I said earlier that the soul and heart are synonymous.

The Soul of Faith

The soul is thought to be the heart of man by many, but in reality, the soul contains the heart of man. It is through the heart that man and God can best communicate. Remember the heart of a man's soul is like his hard drive, his repository of the Word and presence of God, housing his holy of holies.

Faith is a spiritual attribute that expresses the acceptance of God's will. It's initiated and established within the soul of man, not his mind. The mind does, however, have to accept the direction of the soul and operate in accord with the soul. Again, it is the job of the mind to bring options; it is the prerogative of the soul to accept or reject them.

Before and while coming to the point of faith, our minds can be all over the place, but our soul and heart shouldn't. The mind wavers because it has to filter circumstances and situations, but the soul should and indeed must hold firmly to its place of agreement with God and God's will if faith in God is to be established and maintained.

The soul must reject the contrarian images and instructions of the mind that are based on the natural senses and feelings of the body as well as shifting events and circumstances. The soul must do so while holding firm in hope seeing the manifestation of what God said, settling the issue regardless of what may happen, even if it means death.

The confidence of believers in Christ must be based on what God wants, not what we want. That is what having faith in God is. To do that, believers must subordinate their will, feelings, what they see, feel, think, etc., to God's will. God's will is expressed in what He has said and directed them to do. Those directions are usually from the heart, not the head.

Just as the fruit of the Spirit is an expression of the attributes of the Holy Spirit, so is faith in God a work, expression, and characteristic of man's heart towards God. As stated before, true faith in God is realized through establishing a triunity between man's soul, mind, and body to the acceptance, expression, and establishment of God's divine will. Accomplishing that is truly entering into oneness with God.

A Glimpse into the Mind
(Seat of Rational Thought)

The mind is the seat of rational thought and natural awareness. The mind is a sort of transformer that transforms our natural perceptions of spiritual perceptions and spiritual perceptions into natural ones. Through awareness, the mind attaches us to our surroundings, serving as the ex-officio link between the *soulical* and all things natural. In the mind, conclusions are reached on the basis of and in accordance with reason or logic, be it natural or spiritual.

The mind is also a gatherer of intangible resources and information from the natural to be considered by the soul. In the New Testament Greek, it is referred to as *dianoia* (dee-an'-oy-ah), the place of deep thought, imagination, and understanding.

A healthy mind should always reflect the intents of the soul. The mind and soul should always operate in complete oneness, the soul being the mind's proprietor. It is the responsibility of the soul to maintain and bring to the mind order and cohesiveness. If it doesn't, the mind will wander and waver; it will also become vulnerable to natural corrupting influences. It may also create doubts, confusion, and disorder. Under certain conditions, it may become rigid and even develop a sort of resistance or rebellion against the soul. Such a state will be produced if it becomes defiled or corrupted by the evil influences of the wicked one (Satan). A defiled, corrupt mind will make it impossible to have faith in God.

As an aside, it should be noted that man can also communicate with God via his mind, and God too can and does communicate with a man via his mind.

A Glimpse into the Physical Body

(Seat of Subjective Thought)

The physical body: The physical body is that portion of man's being that houses man's corporeal nature. It is the seat of man's subjective thought and natural perceptions, housing his natural senses. Man's physical body makes choices and responds in accordance with its senses. Man's physical body also enables him to exist in and navigate through natural planes of existence.

Man's body pretty much responds to the soul via the mind to do their biddings. It does, however, have memory capabilities throughout, enabling it to respond fluidly to situations, circumstances, its environment, and the tasks it is given to perform.

Again, it should be noted that man can also communicate with God via his physical body, just as God can and does communicate with man via man's physical body. True faith in God is realized through establishing a triunity between man's soul, mind, and body to the acceptance, expression, and establishment of God's divine will.

The Spirit of Life

There is one other aspect to this that we must bring to the table. There is also a spirit in man. For lack of a better way to express this, I will call this the spirit or breath of life. In reality, that's what it does; it empowers and animates not only man but all living creatures that God creates.

The spirit of life is so closely related to man's soul and integrated throughout man that they seem to be one and the same, but they are not. It is like fuel in a vehicle that powers the vehicle, but does not control, influence, or determine its directions.

The spirit of life gives life to everything that man does and will provide the energy that man needs to stand against that which will inevitably come against him in his walk of faith.

Faith Is Spiritual

As said earlier, faith is a spiritual attribute that expresses the acceptance of God's will. It is initiated and established in the soul of man, not his mind. True faith is believing what God said. Religious faith is believing what we think or feel about what God said. Doubt is believing what the devil or the situations and circumstances say and seeking to get man's body to accept it.

True faith is entered into an established agreement. When we enter into a true agreement with God, we enter into oneness with Him on that issue, resulting in unwavering faith in God. Again, true faith is entered into and established through agreement, agreeing with the Spirit of God, or agreeing with the spirit of doubt and unbelief, which is against God. Remember the spirit of doubt and unbelief is one spirit. You will know it is present because it always produces uncertainty and fear. Its intensity determines the level of doubt, unbelief, and, when present, disbelief.

Always remember before and while coming to the point of faith, our minds can be all over the place, but our soul and heart should be fixed. The mind wavers because it has to filter circumstances and situations. The doubt and unbelief seek to influence the mind in order to influence the soul, but the objective is to sow a seed of doubt and unbelief in the soul. The key to staying and walking in faith is for the soul to hold firmly to its place of agreement with God and God's will. It is the tenacity of the soul that established and maintained our faith in God.

The soul must reject the contrarian images of the mind that are based on circumstances and shifting events while holding firm in hope as to the manifestation of what God said, settling the issue regardless of what may happen, even if it means death.

As stated previously, just as the fruit of the Spirit is an expression of the attributes of the Holy Spirit, so is faith in God a work, expression, and characteristic of man's heart towards God. Faith in God is a work of the spirit (soul) of man.

True, unwavering faith in God begins through establishing a triunity between man's soul, mind, and body to the acceptance, expression, and establishment of God's divine will. That process should not be considered complete until all three enter into oneness with each other. Accomplishing that is truly entering into oneness with God. It is the responsibility of the soul of man, not his mind, to establish and maintain that oneness.

CHAPTER 29:

THE FOCUS OF FAITH

Defining Focus

Throughout this book, we have discussed oneness and being focused. Before we go any further, I believe it's important to see how being focused and oneness operate. This, too, will be just a wee bit technical and redundant, but it's necessary to more clearly understand how faith in God is formed within our souls.

Once faith is formed in our hearts (souls), we will not doubt, no matter what we face. One's primary belief takes place in the heart (soul), not the head (mind). Keep in mind that it is with the mind we accept, and it is with the heart we believe.

Let's first look at focus. Focus in the context of this book is the point in which the heart of the believer synchronizes with the will of God; it is the point in which we become one with God.

Naturally, to focus, there has to be a point in which two or more things converge to form a single point of reference. It is at that point oneness and clarity are achieved. It's at that point where things in the natural conform to things in the spiritual to form agreement. This is also the point where the personification of faith is realized. It is also the point in which what takes place in the spiritual realm manifests itself in the natural, sometimes in seed form.

Earlier, I said that the personification of faith is accomplished through the aligning and bringing into agreement and oneness of the believer's hopes, dreams, and desires with God's. The will of God must become the will of the believer for there to be faith in God. In such an instance, oneness in faith is automatic.

Once faith is personified, the believer will believe God, do for God, and go through unimaginable things for God. They will do so because they are one with God. Not *at* one with God but *one* with God. Once the believer enters that place, to deny God will be to deny self. It is also at that point when the believer will have enormous access to the things of God.

It should be the goal for every believer to be one with God. Doing so does not supplant man's will or ability to choose; it does mean, however, that they choose beforehand to live in oneness and perfect harmony with Him. When they do, they choose to choose only those things that will enhance and strengthen their relationship with Him, not diminish it. Doing so does indeed personify the believers' faith in God.

Creating the Focus of Faith

The focus of faith is a God-centered focus. You may ask how that type of focus takes place. What I am about to say may seem to some a little weird since there isn't definitive biblical evidence as to what I am about to share. Consider, therefore, the next few sentences to be conjecture.

(INFORMATION FLOW THROUGH THE BODY)

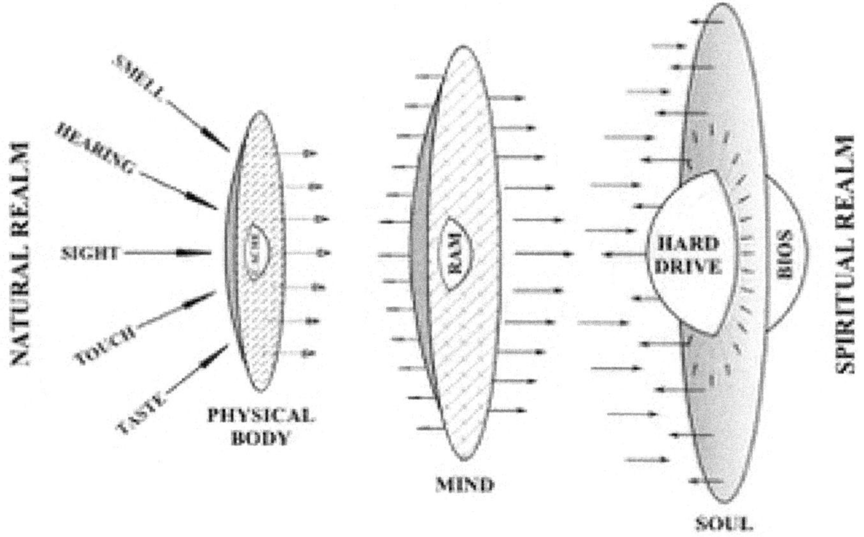

NATURAL SPIRITUAL

First, it's important to note that faith is a factor of what we believe, and what we believe is a factor of what we have accepted as true. For us to believe, there must be something to consider; that's a factor of information received or experiences experienced.

That brings us to how information flows through our body. "Body" in this context is referring to our whole being, not just the physical portion we see when looking in a mirror.

As depicted in the above illustration, information flows in two directions: from spiritual to natural and from natural to spiritual. The acceptance of the information that flows from natural to spiritual will usually produce a carnal mind and, therefore, a carnal-minded person. The acceptance of the information that flows from spiritual to natural will usually produce a spiritual-minded person. Information that flows from spiritual to natural is based on and influenced by the Spirit of God and/or God's Word.

GOD-CENTERED FOCUS

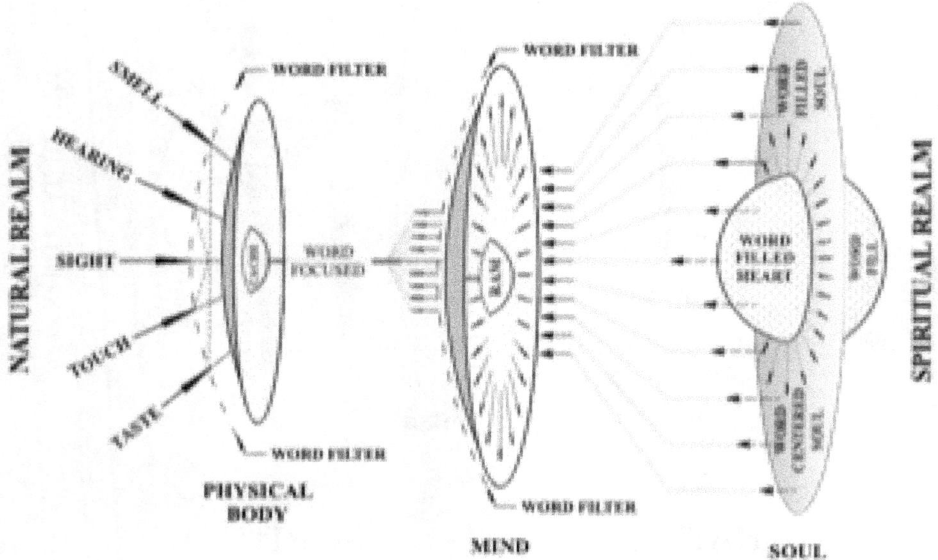

So how does the God-centered focus of faith take place? As depicted above, it starts in the realm of the spirit, filling the heart of the believer with God's Word and the acceptance of the things that are based upon God's Word. All information from the physical body and mind is weighed, vetted, and measured against God's Word. The focus of faith is bringing everything into alignment with what God says or has said. If a person doesn't believe what God said, there cannot be faith in God; there may indeed be confidence, but there will not be faith in God.

For there to be faith in God, that which is in agreement with God's Word is accepted by the soul, and that which is contrary is rejected. If the soul has accepted and affirmed the information of the heart, that affirmation is sent from the soul to the mind, which embraces it, passing it on to the physical body, which reflects through its actions what has been affirmed by the mind and soul. This level of agreement and alignment with God and His Word creates oneness, establishing focus and resulting in faith in God. That faith is then manifested in the physical responses of the outer man.

The key to the focus of faith is making sure that everything that is said, thought, and done is in perfect agreement with God's Word. That level of agreement and oneness with God can only be realized if the person believes God. When they do, they will remain focused and in faith.

As stated previously, faith in God begins in the spiritual realm and by bringing the physical into alignment with what God has said about what is being hoped for. We saw how faith in God is produced and how making sure everything being said or done will ensure that we will remain focused while walking in faith. So with that in mind, let's consider a similar scenario to see how doubt and unbelief are produced.

THE CORRUPT MIND

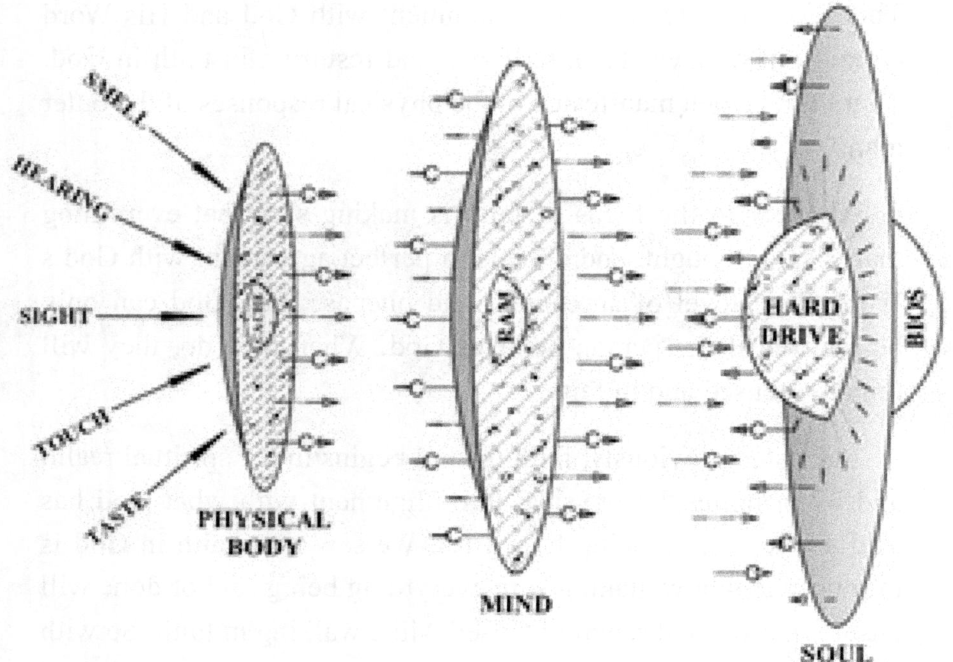

The Corrupted Mind

A carnal-minded person has a heart and soul that is misaligned with or has rejected God. As a result of having no clear word from God, the soul becomes dependent upon the mind for guidance; the mind then becomes dependent upon the physical body relying upon its natural senses. The person then makes choices relying upon the senses that can be less than certain and produce doubt and unbelief in both the mind and soul.

When exercising faith in God, information flows from spiritual to natural. However, when in doubt and unbelief, information flows from natural to spiritual. The carnal person receives a variety of thoughts, feelings, and ideas from the senses; some spawned by situations and circumstances, some by the person's dreams, hopes, desires, etc. Those promptings are then picked up and received by the mind, where they undergo initial filtering. If, however, the mind is carnal, with little to no fidelity or commitment to truth, the information received by the soul will likely be corrupt. If the soul has lost its connection to God and doesn't trust or has rejected God's Word, the person will be carnal and live a life of doubt and unbelief. The person's belief system is sculptured by a natural world that has largely rejected the things of God, replacing God's standards with their own. The things of God may even be repulsive to such a person, which is rejection.

After those thoughts are filtered (some may not be filtered), they are forwarded to the soul for final acceptance or rejection. The situation then is compounded because the soul has no godly standard to use to make judgments. Once those poorly vetted thoughts are received by the soul, there may or may not be an agreement of the soul with the mind. There may only be a loose acceptance that takes place, producing more uncertainty in the body.

The soul then returns to that carnal mind a judgment of uncertainty, or worse, a corrupt sense of certainty. That uncertainty or corrupt sense of certainty will then be reflected in the body, which responds accordingly. As a result of the uncertainty, the body will begin to feel a lack of confidence and certainty throughout. It is that sense of uncertainty that produces feelings of doubt. Depending on the level of uncertainty, the person will not only act in uncertainty and doubt but also in fear and unbelief, depending on the situation. Such a person cannot produce faith in God.

You may have noticed that true faith in God was an impossibility for the carnal person due to a corrupt mind and soul. That corruption occurred because of a heart that was void of God's Word and due to the person having little to no relationship with God. Such a person cannot achieve the focus of faith because there is little to no word to focus upon.

When a person rejects God, they will also empty their heart of the things of God, leaving their heart void of God's Word, leaving themselves vulnerable to that which is evil. Because there is empty space in their heart, the person will usually fill that space with the cares of the world, corrupting their heart. It's impossible for such a person to have the focus of faith or faith in God.

Believers, too, can find themselves in a similar situation when they become too indulgent upon the cares of the world. The cares of the world are corrupting influences. Worldliness will strangle the influence that God's Word has upon their lives resulting in a lack of godliness.

It's worth emphasizing that the soul determines the direction of the whole body. If the soul has embraced a false sense of right and wrong or rejects the things of God, the whole body will be thrust into confusion, darkness, and bondage to sin. Should that occur, it would be unlikely for such a person to reach his or her full potential by not refusing to embrace the mind of God. That's why a God-centered focus is so important.

The God-centered focus of faith is achieved when the mind and soul gather and filter thoughts and ideas received by the senses through God's Word. That filtering process determines what will or will not enter the heart. Once those thoughts and ideas are determined to be in agreement with God's Word, they are sent to the heart and used to create godly outcomes in the life of the believer. The person's actions and life are then at one with God and will exemplify the focus of faith.

That same process is used to develop and establish our sense and standard of right and wrong. Once a standard is accepted, it creates a life's norm. Once that norm is established and settled in the person's soul, it is used to automatically judge whether a thing is acceptable. It then becomes the basis for the person's norms, their natural and normal way of doing, accepting, and rejecting things.

Norms are and should be very difficult to change. This is why it is so important to be careful as to what we accept as facts in our lives. That is also why it is so important to allow truth (God's Word) to be the final determiner of what is right, wrong, acceptable, or unacceptable. Remember what Jesus said in John 8:32 (KJV), "*And ye shall know the truth, and the truth shall make you free.*"

There is no lack of information and opinions in our world today. There simply must be an unwavering, unyielding standard for believers to go to when they want to determine what truly should or should not be embraced. God's word of truth is and must be that standard. It is only God's Word that changes not. There simply is no better standard that men can use as a sure guide for their lives.

THE SPIRITUAL MIND

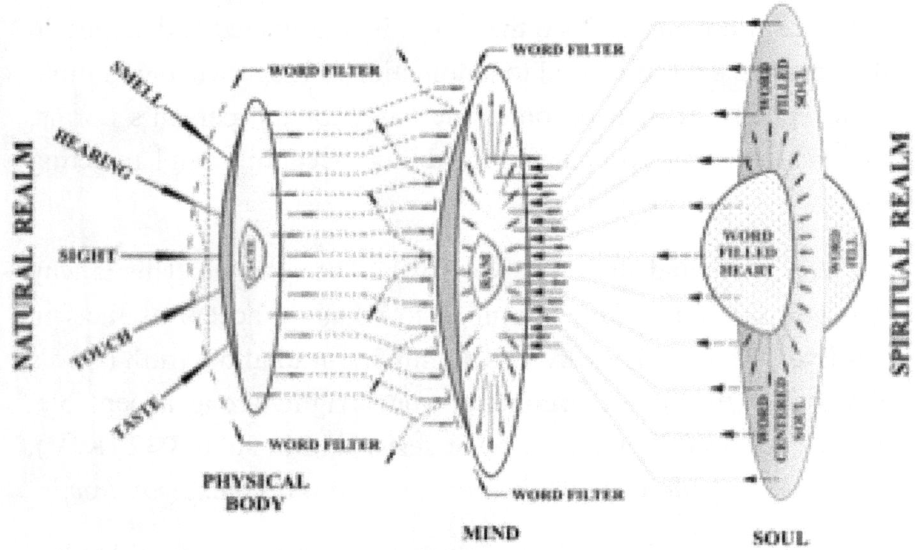

The Spiritual Mind

The previous image illustrates how thoughts, ideas, and perceptions from the senses of the physical body and the mind's own imaginings, flood the mind. A healthy (spiritual) mind rejects outright those things that are in obvious conflict with or are not conducive to the soul's previously (godly) established precedents. Things that are not in agreement with the soul's precedents or that need evaluating are evaluated in the mind where it decides to accept or reject them. The things that are acceptable are sent to the soul for acceptance, and if they are, a directive is given to the body, which acts in accordance with the intents of the heart. The problem comes in when the soul and mind use flawed or misinformation to make decisions.

Predetermined standards based on God's Word should be employed to weigh every choice the mind makes and prevent the mind's deception. The mind will use anything it accepts as truth to make those choices. That is also how norms are developed. God's Word must and should be that predetermined standard. God's Word is truth and is the basis for all truth. It is foolhardy to use anything other than God's Word as the standard to determine what enters the heart and, therefore, one's life.

"Teach me thy way, O LORD; I will walk in thy truth: unite my heart to fear thy name." Psalm 86:11 (KJV)

"Sanctify them through thy truth: thy word is truth." John 17:17 (KJV)

When there is no sure standard of right and wrong, there will be no absolutes, making it easier to be deceived. This is why using the Word of God as the standard for determining what is right and wrong is so important. God's Word does not change; it is a fundamental, foundational norm, making it all but impossible for one to be deceived and making walking in faith all but second nature.

WORD-FILLED HEART

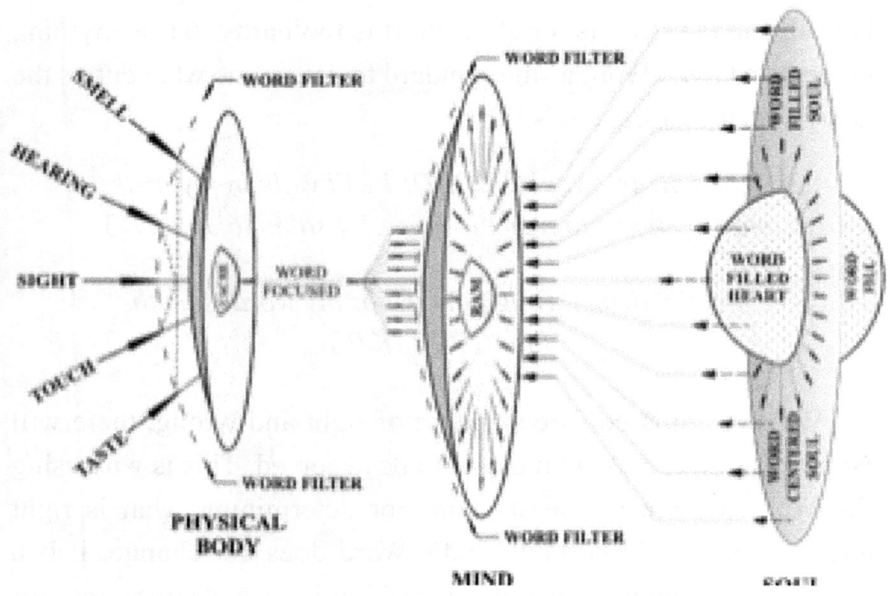

The Word-Filled Heart

The above illustration shows the Word-filled heart. When God's Word is embraced, it becomes the standard and filter through which everything flows through the believer's physical body, mind, and soul. Using God's Word as a standard makes it easier for the mind and, therefore, the soul to filter everything that seeks to enter into and through the mind to get to the soul and thereby to the heart of man. Even the natural senses are brought into proper perspective and alignment when governed by God's Word and not the circumstances the senses bring.

Again, it is the job of the mind to give directives to the physical body and to bring options to the soul. It is the job of the soul to accept or reject the options the mind may or may not bring. That process determines whether or not a person will or will not walk in faith. Again, this is why it is so important to filter everything through God's Word. This is also why it is vitally important to know and accept God's Word as our life's standard and as divine and absolute truth.

Truth doesn't have to be divine, but it does have to be absolute. If one does not consider truth to be as it is indeed absolute, it invites confusion and, therefore, wavering, resulting in unbelief, which produces doubt.

Once a person accepts the belief that truth is not absolute, it is also much easier for that person to be deceived because there is no firm basis for what is right or wrong. Knowing what's right automatically identifies what's wrong. The reverse is also true. It is best, however, to be able to clearly know what's right or wrong.

A lack of absolute truth also eliminates certainty and, therefore, soundness. Such a state of the soul and mind will develop within the person a spongeable belief system. The person's lack of certainty makes them vulnerable to accepting any influence that to them makes sense.

The lack of a commitment to absolute truth is also an indication that the person has either rejected God's Word or has rendered His Word fallible. As a result, the person would have rendered God's Word ineffective as a filter, making them vulnerable to deception, doubt, and unbelief. Once that happens, the person more easily doubts, loses focus, and once that happens, they lose faith. It's impossible to have faith in God, and a God-centered focus is key to doing what Jesus instructed, "Have faith in God."

To have faith in God, one must be focused on God and be as aggressive as necessary to maintain the focus that will be necessary to plow through that which opposes God's will. Faith in God also provides the believer the confidence necessary to give intelligent consideration of what God has done, thereby deducing from that consideration what He can, is, or will do in the situations being faced.

Faith in God also sparks within the person of faith the tenaciousness needed to not give up or give in to the challenges and opposition that will inevitably be faced when believing God. The man or woman of faith will also be and remain in humble submission to the will of God throughout the process. They will not allow their hearts to be moved by the situations and circumstances they face but remain in total, humble obedience, submission, and oneness with God. Doing so is truly having faith in God and is faith made easy.

CHAPTER 30:

THE REST OF FAITH

*"There remaineth therefore a
rest to the people of God."
(Hebrews 4:9, KJV)*

*"For he that is entered into his rest, he also hath
"ceased from his own works, as God did from his."
(Hebrews 4:10, KJV)*

True faith in God always produces a state of rest in God. The function of faith is not to bring us to the place where we would be like a child in a candy store, getting any and everything we want when we want it. True faith in God helps us to realize the promises of God and accomplish His will.

God has promised those that obey Him that, to supply their needs, He will give them the desires of their heart (if they delight themselves in Him); He also promised to give them that which they ask Him if they believe and ask in accordance with His will.

The promises of God are also a reflection and expression of God's will and desire for all mankind. When looking at God's promises, one might ask why God would make such commitments. I submit to you that, as with any parent, it's His love. God does all that He does for man because of His love. There's also another reason, His rest. Scriptures suggest that God has a goal, commitment, and a desire for all those that are His to enter into His rest. God's rest is our place of promise, the place where we realize the things we hope for. The place where we subordinate our will and abilities to receive His favor and access His promises to us.

We cannot truly be in that place while being filled with anxiety, nor can we be filled with faith and anxiety. We must grow into the place where our efforts enable us to enter into His rest, doing so in God's timing, not our own. That is laboring to enter into His rest.

In laboring to enter God's rest, we literally work ourselves out of a job, leaving the *rest* up to God. That's why we must be led by God's Spirit. Simply put, we must do our part, do it right, and do it in accordance with God's timing, then place the rest in God's hands. When we do, we enter into at least the portion of God's rest that is related to that effort.

Before we get too far into the discussion of God's rest. The study of God's rest deserves a book of its own, so I won't get too involved with it in this book. Having said that, consider this chapter to be somewhat of an introduction to that eventual discussion. For now, let's take a glimpse into how faith in God relates to the rest of God.

Faith in God Leads to Rest in God

"And on the seventh day God ended his work which he had made; and he rested on the seventh day from all his work which he had made" (Genesis 2:2, KJV).

"Let us labour therefore to enter into that rest, lest any man fall after the same example of unbelief" (Hebrews 4:11, KJV).

Genesis chapter 2 gives us the pattern for entering God's rest: (1) determine what must be done, (2) devise a plan to do it, (3) execute the plan, (4) finish the work, (5) rest. Put an end to the tinkering, and enjoy what has been created. If the previous were done properly, there is nothing else to be done. Stop working on that which needs no work. If it needs more work, it wasn't finished. It's the same with faith; do the work that should be done, then *be* done with it.

In the book of Hebrews, mainly in chapters 3 and 4, God gives us a glimpse into His desire for His people to enter into His rest.

Rest here is not the taking of ease but rather the taking of leave. Rest must be entered into by completing the task that must be performed. Genesis chapter 2, verse 2 states that God rested on the seventh day. It is also recorded why He rested. God rested not because He was tired or needed a break but because He completed all that he determined to do. He finished His work. The Hebrew word for "rest" in Genesis 2:2 is *shabath* (shaw-bath'). *Shabath* means "to take leave of, to repose, desist from exertion, to still, put away, make to rest…" It is bringing the task to completion. To enter true rest, one must complete the task they have been given to perform.

We cannot enter into rest until we complete the task we've been given to perform. Having said that, I have to explain there is an individual rest and a collective rest that must be entered into. That is why faith without works is dead. Faith will always produce corresponding action (works) because there's always something that must be completed before manifestation. That's also why faith will always be Focused, Aggressive, Intelligent, Tenacious, and Humble. Those attributes are an indication that faith is at work in the midst of every situation and circumstance.

So when walking in faith, always check to see if any or all of these attributes are present in your heart. If they are, you can "rest" assured that faith is present. The greater the level of focus, godly aggressiveness, intelligence, tenaciousness, and humility, the greater the level of faith.

Know this: Faith in God will always produce rest. True faith in God will usher us into the rest of God, at least as it relates to the thing for which we are hoping. If you're exercising faith but don't have rest, there is a lack in your faith in God. You may have confidence, but you do not have the level of faith that will bring you into God's rest, which should be your goal.

Believers must believe God. Self-confidence is not enough. Self-confidence does not equal being God-confident. If you are going to enter into the level of faith that will bring you into God's rest, you must do and complete the works that will bring you into it. Once you have, commit it into God's hands and leave the rest up to Him. You have done your part; now, let God do His. Doing so allows you to enter into God's peace. Peace leads to or produces rest. We should see then how entering into God's rest is a manifestation of our "faith in God."

Remember This: The Difference in Hope and Faith

Hope is inspiration expressed in expectation and desire; faith is confidence expressed in one's trust in God, producing the substance of the thing being hoped for.

CHAPTER 31:

MEASURING FAITH

I previously said that entering into God's rest should be every believer's goal. Unfortunately, it is rarely mentioned in churches today. That's unfortunate because if entering into God's rest should be each believer's goal, little to no information is given to instruct them as to how to do so. If it becomes the believer's goal, they would then have something upon which to focus, and they would know when they would reach one of the highest, if not the highest, levels of faith that can be attained. Yes, there are levels of faith, and there are a few that I am going to introduce to you.

The truth, however, is that there is only one faith, and what I am calling levels of faith is an indicator of the increase or decrease of one's faith at any given point. That increase or decline also parallels our relationship with God at a given point. I imagine this is a bit confusing for some, but follow along a little longer before jumping ship.

There is only one faith because there is only one relationship we should have with God; as our relationship with God grows, so will our faith. The relationship we have with God may differ, but that difference should be due to our gifting, God's will, His plan, and His purpose for us individually and collectively.

Think of this in the context of the relationship that you have with the members of your own physical body. You have one love for your whole body and have one relationship with it; however, you relate to and use each member differently. It is the same with our relationship with God. We are members of His body; He uses each of us and empowers us to do His will. As we allow Him to use us, we become more comfortable and capable, resulting in a greater level of our faith in God. It's like training a part of your body to do something through repetition; eventually, the response becomes reflexive, automatic.

Our faith reflects the growth of our relationship with God. Our faith also reflects our closeness and commitment to God. It's also a reflection of our agreement or disagreement with God and His will. As we draw closer to God, our relationship with God shifts, becoming closer, resulting in greater trust, which results in a greater level of faith in God.

As we draw closer to God, increasing our trust in God, our faith increases, affording us the opportunity to do new, different, and greater things for God. This growth in our relationship with God will or should eventually lead to oneness with God. That place where there's no difference in our will and God's will.

Because faith is relational, faith is also fluid, not stagnant. Too often, believers take an all-or-nothing approach to faith, but they shouldn't. Understanding the levels of faith will give a basis upon which one can determine what level of faith they are on at any given time. This will also help those walking in faith to be focused and remain focused during difficult times.

There is an appropriate application of faith that believers must apply in every area of their life. Faith itself is relatively simple and straightforward, but the appropriate application of faith can be somewhat involved.

The following is only a brief introduction to the various levels of faith that anyone can reach as they grow in their relationship or interactions with God. I have identified ten, including one that is not a level but rather an increase or supplement to the faith everyone already has. I'll clear that up later. The levels of faith are (1) Measure of Faith, (2) Proportional Faith, (3) No Faith, (4) Limited (*Little*) Faith, (5) Weak Faith, (6) Mustard Seed Faith, (7) Great Faith, (8) Extreme Faith, (9) Full of Faith, (10) Transcendent Faith. Let's look at each:

1. Measure of Faith

The measure of faith is a basic level of faith that God gives to everyone. In Romans 12:3 (KJV), Paul lets us know that *"...God hath dealt to every man the measure [limited portion] of faith."* The measure of faith produces various levels of confidence that everyone uses to accomplish the things that they do in their daily life. It's also used to produce the confidence needed for everyone to initiate and develop their personal relationship with God.

Remember true faith in God is always relational. It's impossible to have a thriving relationship with one in whom you have no faith. It is also impossible to have faith in one whom you do not believe exists.

The measure of faith that God gives each of us makes it possible for anyone to have the assurance that God exists and that He will provide one's daily needs. With that basic allocation of faith comes an innate desire to go beyond simply believing that God exists to have a desire to know Him. The believer's desire to know God will become the catalyst for developing an ever-increasing, personal, and intimate relationship with Him. As that relationship increases, so will their faith.

Believers too often settle for remaining on this basic level of faith. They do little to cause their faith to grow. This basic level of faith grows by going through the challenges faced and by seeing God working on their behalf to resolve them. It's important to remember that the measure of faith is given to everyone to start each of us off on the path of exploration of our relationship with God.

As our relationship with God grows, so will our faith in God grow to levels that cannot be imagined. The challenges that we face in life help us to forge a depth and closeness in our relationship with God and foster the growth in our faith in God.

To advance beyond this basic level of faith, each of us must intentionally work on developing our relationship with God and learn to see Him at work in our lives.

2. Proportional Faith

Proportional faith is the level of faith I mentioned earlier as requiring a bit of clarity. Proportional faith is not a level of faith but rather a divine allocation of faith. Proportional faith is an impartation of faith by the Holy Spirit that increases the person's existing level of faith. The person's faith is increased to accomplish a specific mission, task, gifting, or empowerment. It may also be given to get the person out of a situation or circumstance that they are going through. Jesus imparted proportional faith to Peter and Jairus, the ruler of the synagogue *(Matthew 14:28, Luke 8:49–50).*

Jesus imparted to Peter a proportion of faith while walking on water, telling him to come. Peter responded by stepping out of the boat onto the water and beginning to walk to Jesus. Peter accepted Jesus' word of faith and did the impossible but later rejected it, choosing to accept the circumstances, resulting in his failure.

There are times when the Lord seeks to impart to us a proportion of faith through a word of inspiration or thought. That word of inspiration or thought is a seed of faith imparted to us to step out and do what may seem to be impossible.

Jesus imparted to Jairus a proportion of faith while on the way to his home to heal his daughter. Before they got there, Jairus received word that his daughter had died and that there was no longer a need for Jesus. As soon as Jesus heard those words, Jesus imparted faith to Jairus, saying, "Only believe." Jairus did, and his daughter was not merely healed but raised from the dead.

We, too, at times start off believing God to do that which is difficult, but the difficult thing turns into something impossible. Jesus' word to us also is "Only believe." If we do so, we will see God do great things in our life. Peter did the impossible; Jairus believed the impossible, but both did so through a proportion of faith imparted to them. Allow the Lord to do the same in you.

Proportional faith is also imparted by the Holy Spirit to sinners in order for them to accept salvation. It is imparted by believers to others, giving them the assurance needed to accomplish things in their life that they would not be able to accomplish otherwise. Such an impartation will often take place by speaking a word of faith. "*So then faith cometh by hearing, and hearing by the word of God*" (Romans 10:17, KJV). It's important to remember that faith can be imparted, but it must also be accepted and kept.

Proportional faith is also the faith used in the operation of spiritual gifts. Romans 12:6 (KJV) states, "*Having then gifts differing according to the grace that is given to us, whether prophecy, let us prophesy according to the proportion of faith.*"

Through grace, God empowers the believer by His Spirit to do the things that are given to them to be done. He then, through the Holy Spirit, imparts the faith that is needed to believe that God will do the things that need to be done. It is important to remember that God will always impart to us the faith that we need to do and accomplish His Will.

3. No Faith

The *No Faith* level is illustrated in Mark 4:40 (KJV), *"And he said unto them, why are ye so fearful? how is it that ye have no faith?"* People that Jesus described as having "no faith" are people who have rejected or lost even the measure of faith that God has given them. Such a state is often due to a wounded spirit and sometimes a rebellious heart. This can easily be corrected by believing and accepting the word of truth. A person with no faith must also practice obedience. An obedient heart is the most effective way to address a faithless heart.

4. Limited (Little) Faith

Then there's the *Limited (Little) Faith* level. Jesus spoke of this level of faith in Matthew 6:30 (KJV), *"Wherefore, if God so clothed the grass of the field, which today is, and tomorrow is cast into the oven, shall he not much more clothe you, O ye of little faith*?"

The person with limited faith is the person who has a shallow, limited relationship with God. They believe that God can but find it difficult to believe that God will. Their perception of God is distorted. They replace trust in God with a duty to God. They will usually seek religion instead of a personal relationship with God.

The person with limited faith has sporadic confidence in God;

they may believe God for one thing but not another. Because of the limits they placed upon their relationship with God, they fail to see or acknowledge the value and worth that God has bestowed upon them. The person with limited faith limits God's ability to help them through their lack of ability to completely trust Him.

Limited faith can be alleviated by developing a closer, more personal, intimate relationship with God. Through the closeness of a personal, intimate relationship with God, the depth of trust in God increases; as trust increases, a greater, more consistent faith is produced, resulting in an increased level of faith in God.

5. Weak Faith

In Romans 14:1, Paul wrote, "*Him that is weak in the faith receive ye, but not to doubtful disputations.*" (KJV) Being weak in faith is a consequence of a lack of acceptance of God's will, His Word, or His grace. The word "weak" in Romans 14:1 is from the Greek word *astheneo* (as-then-eh'-o), meaning "to be feeble (*in any sense*)." It is to be diseased, sick (Strong's Concordance). The thrust of *astheneo* is not to be inherently weak but to be made weak. As in natural sicknesses, many times, the sickness is due to what we acquire rather than what occurs naturally. The same holds true with weak faith. Weak faith is a result of an existing level of faith being diminished. It is a result of having a type of spiritual malnourishment.

Anytime we exhort our will, customs, religious beliefs, or anything else above God's Word and grace, we diminish our faith in God. In fact, the more we subordinate our relationship with God to the things of the world, the weaker our faith in God will become. Such outcomes can be avoided by making sure that nothing is allowed to take priority over the things of God.

To strengthen weak faith, one must make sure that the things of God always have precedence in every area of one's life. Value God's Word, reject that which is contrary to His Word, develop a taste and desire for His Word. Never place anything above God or His Word; doing so will always weaken your faith.

6. Mustard Seed Faith

The *Mustard Seed Faith* level. Jesus described it in Matthew 17:20 (KJV) when He said, *"...verily I say unto you, if ye have faith as a grain of mustard seed, ye shall say unto this mountain, remove hence to yonder place; and it shall remove; and nothing shall be impossible unto you."* It's easy to confuse the Mustard Seed Faith level with the Little Faith level because of the size of the mustard seed.

When Jesus compared faith to the mustard seed, He was not only talking about the size of the seed but also the greatness of its potential. Mustard seed faith is a faith with explosive potential released over time or as needed to do, accomplish, or create great things.

The key to mustard seed faith is the ability to look beyond what seems to be one's inadequacies in order to do and accomplish great things. That is done by seeing one's self, not through their own eyes or the eyes of others but through the eyes of God.

Like the mustard seed, God has placed an unseen, untapped potential in each of us that is waiting to be unleashed. That unleashing, however, is not done solely by the will of the one with the Mustard Seed Faith but rather in concert with the will of God. This is the message of Paul the Apostle, "*I can do all things through Christ which strengtheneth me*" (Philippians 4:13, KJV).

Faith on all levels is easier to approach when applied through a relationship with God rather than the will of self. With mustard seed faith, it is a must. In the final analysis, it always comes down to placing our faith in God rather than self. If self-confidence alone was enough, we would likely have what we want. The key is "*through Christ.*"

The hidden potential of mustard seed faith is unleashed when applied in agreement with the will of God. This is true with every seed, and it is true with mustard seed faith. As earth and water work with a natural seed to unleash its potential, so it is with mustard seed faith when applied in harmony with God's will. When that happens, that little seed of faith produces great things in and through God.

7. Great Faith

Then there is the *Great Faith* level. Previously, I shared the story of the woman of Canaan in Matthew 15:23–28 (KJV). She came to Jesus, asking Him to heal her daughter that was being vexed with a devil. Jesus told her that He was only sent "*...unto the lost sheep of the house of Israel.*" She persisted, saying, "*Lord, help me.*" He then told her that it wasn't proper to give the child's food to the dogs. Not taking no for an answer, she replied, "... *Truth, Lord: yet the dogs eat of the crumbs which fall from their masters' table.*" Jesus then replied, "*...woman, great is thy faith: be it unto thee even as thou wilt.*" Her daughter was healed.

I first introduced this woman to you to illustrate the aggressiveness of faith. A person with great faith will be focused, appropriately aggressive, intelligent in their efforts to accomplish their objective, relentlessly tenacious, and humble.

The person with great faith doesn't waste their efforts on self-confidence, trying not to doubt that this or that will or not happen. The person with great faith turns their sights squarely on God and His ability to do and act. They personify Numbers 23:19 (KJV), *"God is not a man, that he should lie; neither the son of man, that he should repent: hath he said, and shall he not do it? or hath he spoken, and shall he not make it good?"*

Those with great faith do exactly what Jesus instructed His disciples to do, "Have faith in God." They know that if they could do it by themselves, it wouldn't need to be done because they would have done it. They, like Abraham and all of those who exercise great faith, simply believe that God will honor his word and that He can and will do what he said that He would do.

God had already told Abraham that "*...in Isaac shall thy seed be called*" (Genesis 21:12, KJV); as a result, Abraham did not hesitate when God told him to offer Isaac as a sacrifice. He resolved in his heart that God was going to keep His word, even if He had to raise him from the dead (Hebrews 11:17–11). Abraham had already heard God's word; this woman from Canaan was trying to get Jesus to speak His word. She believed that if He did, her daughter would be healed.

That is the key to great faith: hearing God's word, believing God's word, receiving God's word, and settling for nothing less than the manifestation of God's word in the situations and circumstances of your life.

Great faith is the pursuit of the things of God regardless of the obstacles. It is indeed not taking no as the final answer.

8. Extreme Faith

Then there is the *Extreme Faith* level. Extreme faith is great faith taken to the next level. There came a centurion to Jesus, explaining that his servant was sick of the palsy. Jesus told Him that He would go to his home and heal his servant. The centurion replied, "*Lord, I am not worthy that thou shouldest come under my roof: but speak the word only, and my servant shall be healed*" (Matthew 8:8, KJV). He continued by explaining to Jesus his relationship with authority, concluding that Jesus (because of His authority) needed only to speak the word, and his servant would be healed (Matthew 8:8). Jesus then replied in amazement, "*…I have not found so great faith, no, not in Israel*" (Matthew 8:10, KJV).

I call the centurion's faith extreme faith. Extreme faith is the faith that recognizes and accepts the authority of God to act on one's behalf. This man, like the woman of Canaan, wasn't of the tribe of Israel, but he was able to recognize the use of authority to accomplish a task. He saw Jesus exercising supreme authority, so he asked Him to use it on his behalf. Once Jesus said that He would do what he had asked, that settled it for the centurion. The centurion also understood the power of delegation when operating in and under authority. With that in mind, the centurion knew that Jesus only needed to give the word; from there, it was done.

We, too, can have and exercise that level of faith by simply seeing what God has done and believing that He will do the same for us. Most of the time, our greatest work is simply seeing what God has done, then believing that He will do the same or greater thing for us.

So far, we have seen a range of faith from no faith to a basic measure of faith to a level of faith that was so great that Jesus hadn't seen such a level of faith even in Israel. Now, let's look at the last two levels. These two, in reality, are what believers are thinking of when they talk about faith.

9. Full of Faith

Few times in Scripture do you find individuals described as being full of faith; in fact, there are only two: Stephen and Barnabas. This is not to say that they are the only ones that were full of faith; I'm sure they were not. You may ask: What about Jesus? In fact, Jesus had faith without measure and was the personification of faith, which is another conversation. For the sake of our discussion, I will stick with Stephen only.

There are certain characteristics of a person that is full of faith; they will always be people of great integrity and intelligence. They will also be full of the Holy Spirit, full of power, full of wisdom, fearless, full of God's Word, and totally faithful to the will of God, even unto death. Those characteristics were reflected in Stephen's life from the time he came on the scene in Acts chapter 6 and Acts chapter 7. Stephen serves as our example of the believer that is full of faith in God.

The person that is full of faith operates in faith in every area of life. They live life in humble submission to God and in His will. In fact, consistent humble submission to God is an indication of the person that is full of faith. The person that is full of faith is prepared to make extreme sacrifices on God's behalf. They seek only to please their heavenly Father.

Today, believers too often seek to elevate their will above God's. Most will not think they do, but in fact, they do just that. Invariably, when "believers pray," "believe God," "seek God's will," etc., they do so to address a perceived need, want, or desire in their own life. A person that is full of faith doesn't take such an approach; they put God first. They ask themselves, "What is God's will?" then seek to perform it, subordinating their will to God's.

Those that are full of faith are not concerned with their own needs because they know and have resolved within their heart that God has or will supply their needs. So they, as priests, intercede for others.

Those that are full of faith are in a state of ever-increasing faith. In every area of their life, they believe God with every fiber of their being. They have an inner confidence that if God said it, He will do it; if God has spoken it, He will bring it to pass. One that is full of faith never struggles or wavers in their faith in God.

Being full of faith is a precursor to transcendent faith. It may seem difficult, but it isn't. It requires a complete subordination of self and will to God and His will. As an instrument in the hands of the musician, they release themselves into the hands of God.

Anyone can have the previously mentioned levels of faith, but only a believer can truly be full of faith. Why? Because only a believer can willingly live their life in humble obedience and submission to the will of their heavenly Father.

Only those who are full of faith will live a life that transcends religion to move completely into a relationship with God. They see Him not as God but as Father. They, through their life, personify the will of their heavenly Father. They willingly have given their life to Him for Him to do with it as He will. Their belief in God and commitment to Him permeate every area of their being. That is true faith in God.

10. Transcendent Faith

Lastly, there is a transcendent level of faith that takes place when a believer enters the state of oneness with God. Transcendent faith is relational faith that has reached the point where the believer moves beyond merely believing and trusting in God for outcomes to the place where they merge their will, hopes, desires, and trust with God's. Transcendent faith is the ultimate faith. It is the highest level of faith believers can reach because they enter a place of oneness with God.

Transcendent faith is faith that not only ushers the believer into oneness with God but also into His divine rest. Faith in God should ultimately lead to rest in God, that place in God where personal efforts end, leaving the rest up to God. Remember personal effort is not just stopped but brought to completion; therefore, they come to an end because there is nothing else personally to be done. True rest cannot be truly entered by leaving necessary things left unfinished.

Transcendent Faith Produces Divine Rest

Transcendent faith is the point in which there are no worries about having or not having, doing or not doing, seeing or not seeing. There are no worries about life, death, or any of those things we tend to give so much weight to in this life. Whenever believers get to that place, they are in or are entering the rest of faith. True faith in God will produce a divine rest in God.

The rest of faith is the place where God's will truly becomes the will of the believer. It is the place where God's ways truly become the ways of the believer. In the place of God's rest, each situation and circumstance is transferred from the believer's hands into God's hands.

Again, the rest of God is entered when a believer enters a state of oneness with God. That oneness is the oneness that Jesus prayed for in John 17:1–26 on behalf of every believer.

Every believer is instructed to "*…labour therefore to enter into that rest…*" (Hebrews 4:11, KJV). This scripture is letting us know that there is something that each of us must do to enter God's rest. The main thing that must be done is to finish the work. There is always something that must be done to see the manifestation of the things you are "hoping for." Always do your part, do it right, do it completely and timely.

As previously stated, rest is realized by diligently completing the work given to be done, not merely stopping. Rest is not entered because you are tired or you have decided to give up. True rest is realized because you have finished your work. Please don't think that God will understand your giving up before you finish doing your part. Who will do it if you don't? Who will do their part while they are doing yours? It could even go undone. Rest cannot be entered into without your enemies defeated, your tasks performed, and your work done.

The children of Israel did not enter the promised land because they stopped in their wilderness. It was there that they rebelled against Moses and God, refusing to confront their enemies. When they finally entered, forty years later, they did not remove all of the indigenous people from the land, which they were to do little by little. Their refusal to fully obey God was evidence of their lack of faith in God and resulted in them never entering the rest that God planned for them and their families.

Today's Christians too often do the same thing; they often refuse to obey God or do so only partially. Partial obedience is total disobedience and reflects one's faith and relationship with

God. Too often, we use faith as a get-out-of-jail-free card or as a means of avoiding trouble or getting out of trouble. Faith is better used to power through and to get through that by which we are challenged, placing it under our feet. If we do that one thing, we will never have to face those things again, and we will be at rest in that area.

We should always labor to enter into rest. Our faith in God will give us that which we need to do so. When the need is to be focused, we will be focused. When the need is to be aggressive, we will be appropriately aggressive. We will also operate intelligently in all that we do because our way will be His way, our will, His will, etc. When we must be tenacious, we will be tenacious, and in all we do, we will remain in humble obedience to God, seeking to do His will, not our own. Doing those things is true faith in God, and having faith in God is truly *Faith Made Easy*.

Words to Ponder

Grace is God's empowerment of us to act; faith is our confident belief in God that He will act and do so in our best interest. Our faith reflects our relationship with God. As our relationship with God grows, so will our trust in God. As our trust in God grows, so will our faith in God grow to levels that are unimaginable.

Faith doesn't have to be that illusive emotional attribute that causes a constant struggle. We can simply place our faith in God. We can simply trust and believe that He will do what He said that He would do. That is truly faith made easy.

And Jesus answering saith unto them, Have faith in God. For verily I say unto you, That whosoever shall say unto this mountain, Be thou removed, and be thou cast into the sea; and shall not doubt in his heart, but shall believe that those things which he saith shall come to pass; he shall have whatsoever he saith. Therefore I say unto you, What things soever ye desire, when ye pray, believe that ye receive them, and ye shall have them. Mark 11:22–24 (KJV)

Our F.A.I.T.H. in God will always produce in our lives Focus, appropriate Aggressiveness, Intelligence, Tenaciousness, and Humility.

Doing so is truly having faith in God, and it is truly *F.A.I.T.H. Made Easy*.

ABOUT THE AUTHOR

Pastor Dr. LaRon D. Bennett Sr., DD, and his wife, Angela, are the founders and pastors of Christ's Church for the End Times, Inc., a non-denominational teaching ministry in Brunswick, Georgia. The goal and thrust of the ministry are to prepare God's people for life and ministry during the times in which we live.

Dr. Bennett and his wife are also the owners of SideView Concepts/BBFCS, Inc., a project management and design firm. The firm also has a separate division that specializes in family and life counseling services.

Dr. Bennett's background in the construction and design fields gives him a unique ability to view the scriptures with spiritual depth and technicality that reveals the scriptures in ways that can be innovative, interesting, and insightful.

He accepted Christ at the age of nineteen and received his ordination through the Miracle Deliverance Church Incorporated of Columbus, Georgia, founded by his now-deceased pastor and mentor, apostle Horace Leonard.

He received an earned Doctor of Divinity degree from Wings Of Faith Bible College of Brunswick, Georgia, where he received the college's 2010–2011 Presidential Award.

Dr. Bennett and his wife, Angela, have been married for more than forty-two years at the time of the publishing of this book. They have three children: their oldest, Erreka J. Bennett, and two sons, LaRon Jr. (Kali Bennett, educator) and Byron (Lauren) Bennett, his youngest. They have five grandchildren, Angelina, Gabriel, Malachi, Naomi, and Micaiah.